There by Design

Field Archaeology in Parks and Gardens

Papers presented at a conference organised by the
Royal Commission on the Historical Monuments of England
and the Garden History Society

Edited by

Paul Pattison

ROYAL
COMMISSION
ON THE HISTORICAL
MONUMENTS
OF ENGLAND

BAR British Series 267
1998

Published in 2016 by
BAR Publishing, Oxford

BAR British Series 267

There by Design: Field Archaeology in Parks and Gardens

ISBN 978 0 86054 880 5

Published in association with the Royal Commission on the Historical Monuments of
England at the National Monuments Record Centre, Kemble Drive, Swindon SN2 2GZ

Volume editor: David Davison

BAR Publishing is the trading name of British Archaeological Reports (Oxford) Ltd.
British Archaeological Reports was first incorporated in 1974 to publish the BAR
Series, International and British. In 1992 Hadrian Books Ltd became part of the BAR
group. This volume was originally published by Archaeopress in conjunction with
British Archaeological Reports (Oxford) Ltd / Hadrian Books Ltd, the Series principal
publisher, in 1998. This present volume is published by BAR Publishing, 2016.

Printed in England

BAR
PUBLISHING

BAR titles are available from:

BAR Publishing
122 Banbury Rd, Oxford, OX2 7BP, UK
EMAIL   info@barpublishing.com
PHONE   +44 (0)1865 310431
FAX   +44 (0)1865 316916
www.barpublishing.com

CONTENTS

FOREWORD

This volume is a collection of ten papers from twelve given at a conference organised by the Royal Commission on the Historical Monuments of England and the Garden History Society, at the Scientific Societies Lecture Theatre in London, on 29 November 1996. Its subject is an archaeological one, concentrating on the contribution made by non-intrusive fieldwork studies to the archaeology of parks and gardens and, in turn, to garden history. The papers are set out here in the order delivered at the conference.

The conference was organised in a climate of ever-growing interest in both the study of garden history and in the restoration of historic parks and gardens. In putting together a programme, our purpose was not to concentrate on excavations or restorations. Rather, it was to bring together a wide audience, both general and specialist, and put before them a series of case studies of regional and national importance which would illustrate the wealth of surviving field evidence – much of it still undiscovered or misunderstood. In doing so, study techniques would be explored and the often pivotal role of field evidence in interpretation articulated.

The opening paper by Chris Taylor stimulated thought about the relationship between archaeology and garden history, more particularly between archaeologists and garden historians and also about the dissemination of the results of archaeological fieldwork. This collection of papers is a small contribution towards furthering links and understanding between the two related disciplines.

The preparations for a conference for some 250 people are not inconsiderable and I am deeply grateful for the help and support of Trevor Pearson, Una Sanderson, Moraig Brown, Al Oswald and Peter Topping for ensuring a successful day. The conference was initiated at the suggestion of Roger Leech and Chris Dunn and was helped along its course by Humphrey Welfare. From the Garden History Society, Roger White, David Lambert and Keith Goodway provided much needed advice and practical help. Harriet Jordan made a fine debut as a conference chairperson, for which I offer my thanks.

In the preparation of these proceedings I am particularly grateful to Trevor Pearson who designed and implemented its style and format, and Moraig Brown who assisted. Una Sanderson assisted with the preparation of the bibliography and Robin Taylor and Diane Williams provided editorial advice and input.

And finally, to all the speakers, many thanks.

Paul Pattison
January 1998

LIST OF CONTRIBUTORS

Mark Bowden   *RCHME Swindon*

C Stephen Briggs   *RCAHMW Aberystwyth*

Graham Brown   *RCHME Swindon*

Paul Everson   *RCHME Swindon*

Graham D Keevill   *Oxford Archaeological Unit*

Neil Linford   *English Heritage: Ancient Monuments Laboratory*

Paul Pattison   *RCHME Cambridge*

John Phibbs   *Debois Landscape Survey Group*

Christopher Taylor   *Archaeological consultant*

Tom Williamson   *Centre for East Anglian Studies*

Robert Wilson-North   *RCHME Exeter*

ABBREVIATIONS

AP   *Air photograph*

CCW   *Countryside Commission for Wales*

EDM   *Electro-magnetic distance measurement*

EH   *English Heritage*

GHS   *Garden History Society*

GIS   *Geographical Information System*

HCA   *Highclere Castle Archives*

HRO   *Hampshire Record Office*

ICOMOS   *International Council on Monuments and Sites*

MAFF   *Ministry of Agriculture, Fisheries and Food*

NMR   *National Monuments Record*

NRO   *Norfolk Record Office*

OS   *Ordnance Survey*

PPG   *Planning Policy Guidance*

RAF   *Royal Air Force*

RCAHMS   *Royal Commission on the Ancient and Historical Monuments of Scotland*

RCAHMW   *Royal Commission on the Ancient and Historical Monuments of Wales*

RCHME   *Royal Commission on the Historical Monuments of England*

RHS   *Royal Horticultural Society*

SRO   *Somerset Record Office*

VCH   *Victoria County History*

WHGT   *Welsh Historic Gardens Trust*

LIST OF ILLUSTRATIONS

FROM RECORDING TO RECOGNITION
Christopher Taylor

ABSTRACT

The primary objective of field archaeologists working on parks and gardens is to discover, record and understand the relict features relating to those parks and gardens. Over the last two decades or so this has been realised by the RCHME and others with a considerable degree of success. A formidable body of experts and expertise has grown up and it is now relatively simple to identify the remains of former parks and gardens, or relict features within existing ones.

Of equal importance is the need to disseminate the results of this work to scholars whose interest in and ability to understand the niceties of field archaeological techniques is inevitably limited. This second objective has not been achieved as successfully as the first; not because of any lack of enthusiasm for the results of field archaeology on the part of garden historians, for they have, on the whole, been quick to grasp the significance of fieldwork results when they have been presented in a readily comprehensible form. Such failures as there have been in this respect lie with the field archaeologists themselves. What is required is not just interpretation and analysis but an overall assessment with the placing of sites in their relative regional, national and historical contexts, in a widely disseminated and clearly understandable form.

Analytical field archaeology is one of the oldest, if not the oldest, forms of archaeological investigation with a history that stretches back into the 16th century (Ashbee 1972, 38–69). The field archaeology of gardens is a much more recent development. Although relict gardens were noted in the late 19th century and the first sites were recorded as early as the 1920s, it was not until the 1960s that the discipline can really be said to have begun. The first major group of relict gardens was published in 1968 (RCHME 1968, lxii) and since then increasing numbers of sites have been found, surveyed and in some cases published (eg Everson 1991; Everson, Taylor and Dunn 1991, 54).

On the whole analytical fieldwork on relict gardens has been successful for a number of reasons. First, it has tried to bring to the notice of garden historians the potentially vast numbers of such gardens. As a result it has widened the sources of evidence for garden history. Second, it has shown that the detailed analysis of these remains can greatly assist the understanding of the history of garden design in that it has revealed numerous examples of elaborate and complex layouts unaltered by later changes.

Third, fieldwork has led to the discovery and recording of a large number of garden remains of the 16th century and later which were either significant at the time of their construction or contain features unknown in the contemporary literature. These gardens include Lyveden of 1590 (Brown and Taylor 1973), Holdenby of the 1580s (Fig 1; RCHME 1981, Holdenby (3, 4 and 5)), both in Northamptonshire, Tackley, Oxfordshire, of the 1620s (Whittle and Taylor 1994), Stowe Barton, Devon, of the 1680s (Wilson-North 1993), and Combs Hall, Suffolk, of 1724–30 (Martin and Oswald 1996).

Fourth, fieldwork has given new insights into well-known gardens by the identification of hitherto unrecognised or unappreciated features. Amongst these gardens are Munstead Wood, Surrey (Everson 1995) and Hall Barn, Buckinghamshire (see below). In addition, because of the wider involvement of analytical fieldwork with all periods of the past and of all relict features, it has led to the discovery of a number of small medieval gardens, of a type hitherto unknown except from documentary or illustrative sources. Amongst the examples recorded, Linton, Cambridgeshire (Brown and Taylor 1991), Cawood, Yorkshire (Blood and Taylor 1992), Nettleham, Lincolnshire (Everson, Taylor and Dunn 1991, Nettleham (1)) and Tintagel, Cornwall (Rose 1994) have all extended considerably knowledge of the varying forms of medieval gardens. More recently, the methods of analytical fieldwork have led to the discovery of what have been termed medieval designed landscapes, ranging in date from the 12th to the 15th centuries and again of very differing forms. These include Shotwick, Cheshire (Everson this volume), Somersham, Cambridgeshire (Taylor 1989), Stow,

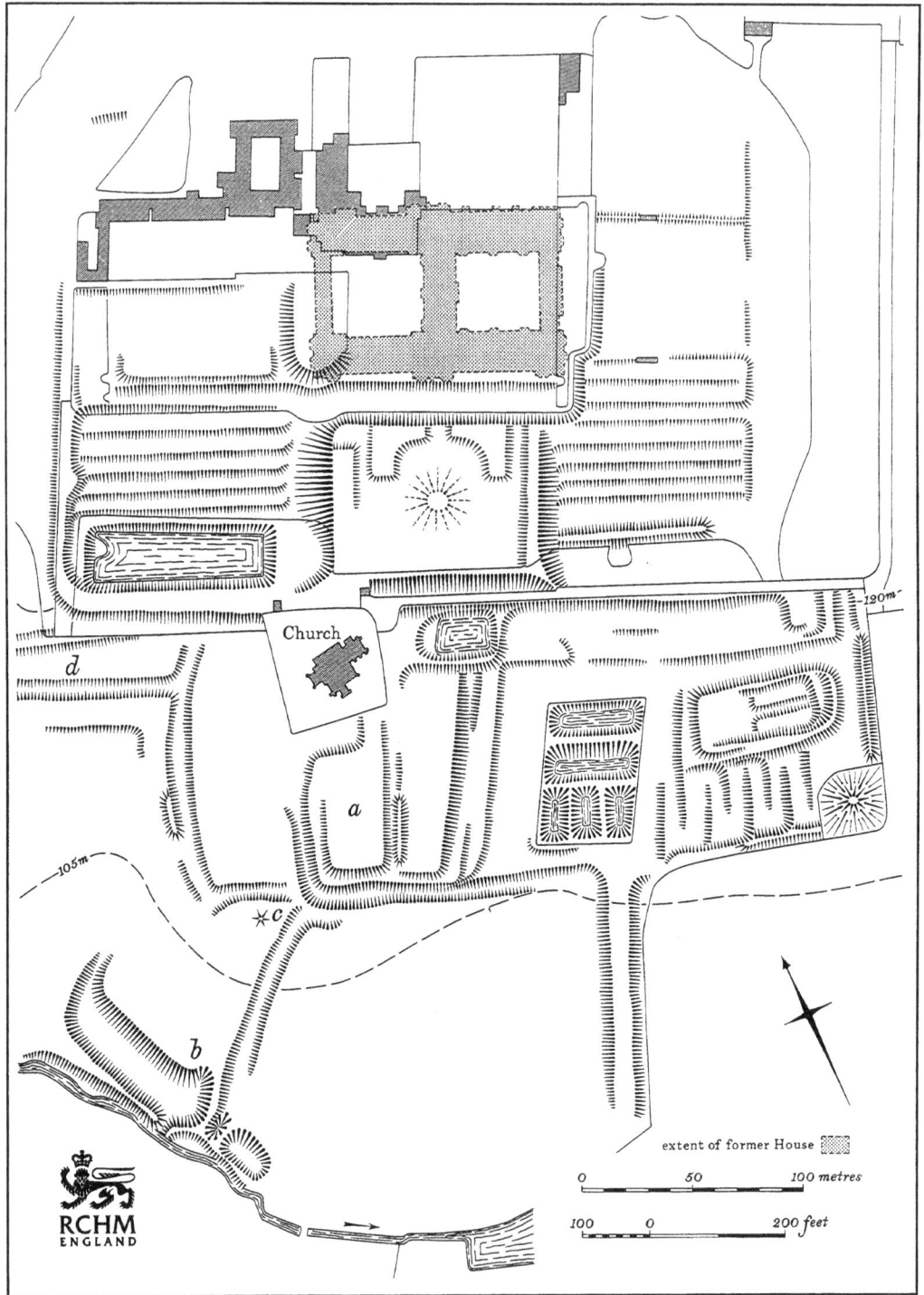

Figure 1
*Plan of the late 16th-
century garden at
Holdenby,
Northamptonshire
(RCHME,© Crown
copyright).*

Lincolnshire (Everson, Taylor and Dunn 1991,
Stow (3 and 4)) and Bodiam, Sussex (Everson
1996c), among many others. Yet another value
of analytical fieldwork has been the confirmation
of the dynamic nature of gardens by the recording of complex palimpsests in some relict examples, such as at Oldstone, Devon (Pattison 1992).

Finally, and of wider significance than simply
for garden history, the results of field archaeology have shown landscape historians that relict
gardens can form parts of highly complex and
dynamic landscapes extending over many centuries. Examples are at Steeple Gidding, Cam-

bridgeshire (Brown and Taylor 1977) and Stainfield, Lincolnshire (Everson, Taylor and Dunn
1991, Stainfield (1-3)).

These are among the successes of analytical
field archaeology in relation to gardens. But
there have also been failures. The principal problem has been the collection of large quantities of
information on relict gardens but with little or no
associated attempts to understand it except at the
most simplistic level. In part, this has been due
to the very nature of archaeology in the late 20th
century. For modern archaeology as a whole is
obsessed with the collection of data. There are

good reasons for this. Most of today's professional archaeologists have grown up in a world of almost continuous destruction of the archaeological heritage as a result of the demands of late 20th-century life. Sites of all periods are always under threat from damage or destruction and time and resources for their study are always limited. Thus there has developed a justifiable philosophy which deems the recovery of information before destruction and its subsequent storage in an archive to be the primary task and the analysis of this information to be a secondary and less important later job. Yet although this philosophy has been imposed by outside pressures it has had unfortunate effects on the understanding of the past. One such effect is that in the rush to gather information – any information – few ask whether it is actually worth gathering at all, or whether the limited resources available might not be better used for the collection of more significant information from elsewhere. Further, although the collection of information is obviously important, just as important is the need to understand it when it has been acquired. Without understanding, information is useless.

It is not just field archaeologists who work in this way. Most professional archaeologists these days spend more time collecting information than trying to analyse it. Anyone who has been involved in the workings of PPG 16 knows this only too well. That this obsession with collecting information is widespread throughout British archaeology may be seen in a recent paper on the understanding of the later Bronze Age by Professor Bradley. He writes, 'To be blunt, we are much more effective at collecting data than we are at analysing information' (Bradley 1996, 38).

However, field archaeologists have been particularly prone to collecting information about gardens rather than trying to interpret it. This is partly because the subject of garden archaeology is relatively new and, as with all new studies, there is an inevitable tendency to be so amazed by what is found that its practitioners forget to ask what is significant. But there is also another reason. The field archaeology of gardens is only a small part, and perhaps not a very important one at that, of the very much wider, older and more developed subject of garden history. Archaeologists tend sometimes to be rather afraid of garden historians, especially when the latter discuss, say, the relationships between 18th-century parklands and the contemporary literature, or the degree of theatrical symbolism in late 16th-century gardens, or the importance of the planting schemes of Gertrude Jekyll. Field archaeologists are very good at recording and analysing Neolithic causewayed camps, Iron Age hillforts, Roman settlements or deserted medieval villages. More importantly, if they are reasonably competent archaeologists, they can understand and discuss the significance of such sites in terms of prehistory, the Roman period or medieval times. That is, they know who is going to use their information, conclusions and ideas about sites of these types and dates. They also understand the background, philosophy, methodology and jargon. And readers of work by field archaeologists – mainly other archaeologists – can understand the language, methods and systems of recording used by these fieldworkers.

Now most field archaeologists are also very good at recording and interpreting relict gardens but they are often not so adept at setting these gardens in their overall context. This is partly because garden history is concerned with aspects of man's interaction with nature, which ultimately produces gardens and designed landscapes that cannot be deduced or understood using the information available to archaeologists from field survey. At the same time, many garden historians would regard the information recoverable by field archaeological techniques as interesting but perhaps somewhat marginal to the wider history of gardens. This is a pity, for the field archaeology of gardens has much to offer garden history, if only the historians and the archaeologists could communicate better. Some of the difficulties of communication certainly lie at the door of the archaeologists and at a very practical level. One example is the method of depiction and the form of expression used by many archaeologists when working on relict gardens. Many garden historians will not, probably quite reasonably, understand what seems to them to be largely incomprehensible descriptions of earthworks or crop and soil marks, the significance of which has to be teased out of complex accounts of multi-phase landscapes. Or, worse still, grasped from mysterious illustrations seemingly made up of lines of regimented tadpoles, which are the accepted archaeological way of presenting the results of such work (Fig 1). Thus a priority is for archaeologists to create simpler illustrations and less involved descriptions in explaining their work to non-archaeologists (but see Pattison; Everson; Bowden this volume).

But communication is also difficult for another and more complex reason. This is that field archaeologists, in what is a relatively new form of study, have not really decided exactly what they should be recording and analysing and why it might or might not be significant. That is they often lack the confidence or knowledge to properly assess in terms of garden history the value of the relict gardens they discover. So they tend to go on recording more and more sites as if they were all equally important and so avoid making proper judgements. Yet as the subject develops this will not do. The field archaeology of gardens may be relatively new but certain features of the subject are now abundantly clear. These include the fact that the remains of former gardens are one of the commonest types of archaeological site in Britain. That relict gardens can range in size from great gardens of royal palaces to humble vegetable plots of agricultural workers. That the remains of gardens of every period from Roman times to the 1970s survive as relict features. And that these remains often lie inextricably mixed up with former villages, field systems, religious sites and castles as well as with country houses. It is also certain that many more will be discovered, not only on the ground but as yet unrecognised within existing sites and monuments records. It is no accident that the English Heritage list of Scheduled Ancient Monuments of national importance contains over a hundred sites of former gardens, variously described as moats, manor house sites, deserted villages, windmill mounds, monastic sites and even prehistoric hillforts, all misidentified or misunderstood.

Yet are garden historians aware of all this? They may well be but not to judge by the material cited by those garden historians in publications on garden history. The mass of evidence which field archaeologists have gathered over the last thirty years or so is still virtually ignored. A few well-known examples occur again and again in the literature. The site of the late 17th-century garden at Harrington in Northamptonshire is one example. It has now been published at least six times and although it is spectacular neither its exact date nor its creator are known for certain and thus its significance is limited. The arrangement of moats, ponds and access ways at Bodiam Castle in Sussex is another. It is frequently cited as the great example of a late medieval designed landscape. Yet while it is certainly important, it is actually by no means typical of its kind or period.

THE FUTURE

So what is to be done by field archaeologists to assist garden historians and advance garden history? First, field archaeologists must decide which of the hundreds of relict gardens that are now known, as well as those still to be discovered, are really important and thus require detailed recording, analysis and publication. Some can be left, at least for the time being, and might just survive for the next generation of scholars to investigate. For, as with many other sites in archaeology today, not every relict garden can be fully examined. Some will have to be ignored or their existence merely noted and decisions, however unpalatable, about what can and should be studied will have to be made. If this is not done, the sites that are really significant for garden history will probably be lost without being understood and preserved if necessary. For example, the remarkable late 13th-century designed landscape at Clun Castle, Shropshire – important for its location and layout and also for its builder, its date and similarity to other contemporary de-

signed landscapes – was first noted in June 1950 (Cambridge University Committee for Aerial Photography, RAF/A/212-236). But its significance was not appreciated until the late 1980s by which time the site had been largely destroyed (Stamper 1996, 8, plate 4).

The criteria for significance of relict gardens should include not only purely archaeological factors such as complexity of remains, state of preservation, potential for future excavation and palaeo-botanical research but also the relevance of its layout, owners, designers, location and other historical factors at both local and national level. Examples of the type of remains which might be regarded as coming into this category of historical significance and which all require detailed field survey and analysis include the following.

Hamels, Hertfordshire

Hamels is an apparently undistinguished landscaped park. Part of it is now ploughed up and what remains is occupied by the inevitable golf course. Yet it contains an almost complete pre-park medieval landscape including the remains of roads, tracks and field systems, while the survival of many hedgerow trees on their banks puts the park into Rackham's class of 'pseudo-parks' (1986, 129). It also has the remains of a late 16th or early 17th-century formal garden, the paths and parterres of which are visible as slight earthworks, while the foundations of its external walls, gate piers and gazebos can still be seen as parchmarks. In addition, there are traces of a late 17th-century wilderness, of 18th and 19th-century pleasure gardens and of a derelict mid 20th-century garden. The significance of Hamels is that it is an exceptionally well-preserved palimpsest of a total landscape as well as a relict garden.

Ebberston, Yorkshire

Ebberston Hall was designed by Colen Campbell in 1718 for William Thompson, MP for Scarborough, as a summer holiday home for Thompson and his mistress. The remains of the contemporary garden which include walkways, a miniature canal and cascades are much damaged and in very poor condition. But what still exists of the original form is a rare survival (Oswald 1954; Pevsner 1966, 154; Hussey 1967, 65–9).

The Pleasance, Kenilworth, Warwickshire

This is a well-known and protected site, which is part of a much wider medieval designed landscape, dating from the early 15th century and apparently built by Henry V as an isolated garden retreat at the far end of the Great Mere (Fig 2). The moated enclosure was linked to the mere by

Figure 2
*The Pleasance,
Kenilworth Castle,
Warwickshire
(Cambridge University
Committee for Aerial
Photography, AMX 89).*

a short canal which terminated in a dock, indicating that the main access to the site was by water. There are documentary references to temporary structures being set up in the interior but the ground evidence indicates the existence of stone corner towers, walls, at least one other permanent structure and some possible flower beds. Its significance lies in its royal connection, its firm date, its place as part of a wider designed landscape and the undocumented structural details in its interior (VCH 1951, 134–6; Colvin 1963, 682–5; Thompson 1964; Thompson 1991, 6, 29).

Stokesay Castle, Shropshire

The castle and its immediate environs are an English Heritage guardianship site, well preserved and beautifully presented, with a reasonably documented history. The surrounding farmland contains the remains of numerous features which may be part of a late medieval designed landscape perhaps contemporary with the construction of the castle. Together with the completely indefensible 'castle' encompassed by a narrow moat, the site consists of a large lake and two groups of ponds, all carefully placed so as to be visible from the window seats of the South Tower, as well as other earthworks which include the site of a probable orchard. Stokesay is important but not just as yet one more late medieval designed landscape among many. Its significance lies partly in the fact that it is in an area which in the late 13th century was only then emerging from Marcher warfare, and that it was

probably laid out not by a great feudal lord but by a merchant, albeit one of the richest in England. It is also important because it is contemporary with a group of similar designed landscapes, including Leeds Castle, Kent, which was probably laid out by the king, for whom the owner of Stokesay, Lawrence of Ludlow, worked. It is possible that Lawrence of Ludlow may have seen Leeds (Munby 1993, 10, 34).

Somerleyton, Suffolk

An impeccably cared for and much visited private garden, laid out in 1844–62, in part perhaps by W A Nesfield. The formal garden, west of the house, has inevitably been simplified in recent times but retains much of the original mid 19th-century arrangement preserved as slight earthworks amongst the existing flower beds. Its significance lies both in the well-preserved nature of what is probably the original Nesfield layout and also in the origins, status and ultimate disgrace of its owner, Sir Samuel Morton Peto (EH 1985).

These are just a few among many sites which would repay archaeological field survey and analysis. But there is another, much easier task for archaeologists which would further garden history. This is to go through existing archives and to publish those sites of relict gardens, already recorded and analysed in full, which may be regarded as historically significant. Examples of this type of site include the following, the records of which are held in the NMR.

Wing, Buckinghamshire

The gardens created here by the Earls of Carnarvon are perhaps the best preserved and certainly the most elaborate of any surviving early to mid 17th-century relict gardens in England. The remains include massive terracing, a canal and some very unusual flower beds of a hitherto undocumented form (VCH 1925, 450 – 1).

Horseheath Park, Cambridgeshire

The remains of this site were recorded during the process of total destruction. The methodology of the recording is of some interest but the principal value of Horseheath is that the survey produced the only modern plan of a garden designed by Roger Pratt to go with the remarkable house he built there in the 1660s. The publication of this plan would be a significant addition to knowledge of late 17th-century gardens. The survey also produced evidence of later modifications there by William Kent (Parsons 1948; VCH 1979, 72).

The Moot, Downton, Wiltshire

This is an undated and undocumented early 18th-century garden which is a miniature version of the amphitheatre and lake at Claremont, Surrey. It was created by the adaptation of a medieval castle mound and the modification of the banks of its bailey (EH 1987b).

Hall Barn, Buckinghamshire

A well-known and well-recorded existing garden, the significance of which has long been appreciated. A recent survey has indicated that it is a more complex garden, and one which extended over a much longer period of time than hitherto realised. In addition to its importance in the late 17th century through its owner and John Evelyn, and in the early 18th century through its links with John Aislabie and thus with Studley Royal, it is now clear that there was also an arrangement of some interest dating from the early 17th century (EH 1987a).

CONCLUSION

These are some of the sites in the national archive, the exact details of which remain unpublished. It is now axiomatic in archaeological circles that such archives are a form of publication. While this may well become the case one day, at the present time scholarly practice lags far behind technological possibilities. Even if the archives are consulted and the very detailed records, including those of the above examples, used, most readers will find it very difficult to divine the importance of the individual gardens on the basis of what is there.

The need for better targeted surveys and for publication and analysis of surveys already executed are just two instances of the ways in which field archaeology can contribute to the advancement of garden history. There are others, some more difficult and involving the changing of long-held practices and beliefs, some easy and requiring only the will and a little effort. The recently published *Garden Archaeology Newsletter* by English Heritage (Howes 1997) is a good example of the latter and a fine instance of ensuring the flow of relevant information from garden archaeologists to garden historians. Much remains to be done along these lines but the rewards for garden history will be immense.

ACKNOWLEDGEMENT

The author wishes to thank Anne Rowe for introducing him to the park at Hamels and for allowing him to use material on it in advance of the publication of her own research.

PARKLANDS AS GUARDIANS OF EARLY LANDSCAPES: HIGHCLERE CASTLE, HAMPSHIRE

Graham Brown

ABSTRACT

Highclere is probably best known for the landscape park created during the 18th and 19th centuries. However, relatively little was known about the earlier landscape until the recent archaeological survey and field investigation undertaken by the RCHME. This work, supplemented by documentary evidence and research by Southampton University, casts a new light on the landscape development at Highclere and shows that, despite the later modifications of the 18th and 19th centuries, large areas of the park contain elements of the medieval and earlier landscapes.

INTRODUCTION

Highclere Castle, the home of Lord Carnarvon, lies in northern Hampshire approximately 20 miles (32 km) from the county town of Winchester and some 4 miles (6.5 km) south of Newbury. The landscape park is considered of national importance and is listed as Grade I in the English Heritage *Register of Parks and Gardens* (EH 1984, 46). It is an area of great contrasts; to the north it is densely wooded while in the south, from Dunesmere Lake, the park retains a planned appearance which has developed over the past 250 years.

The importance of Highclere as a landscape park and garden is amply demonstrated by 19th-century commentary. William Cobbett, writing in 1821, says:

> *I came from Burghclere this morning, through the park of Lord Carnarvon at Highclere ... This is, according to my fancy the prettiest park that I have ever seen. A great variety of hill and dell ... I like this place better than Fonthill, Blenheim, Stowe, or any other gentleman's grounds that I have seen (1912, 7).*

A few years later Lady Grenville sent her gardener to Highclere to look at 'the beautiful American garden and learn more about azaleas which are Lord Grenville's passion' (HCA Family letters Vol 2, 19). In the *Gardening Magazine* of 1834 (Vol X, 257), although an author criticised some aspects of the estate, nevertheless, he was particularly impressed by the natural beauty of the place with the careful planting of trees and noted that, in his opinion:

> *there is no place in England where so much dignity of character, so much elegant variety, and so much cultivated beauty, is preserved throughout a place of such great extent.*

The first archaeological investigation at Highclere can be traced to J Williams-Freeman, when preparing his volume on the earthworks of Hampshire (1915, 90). In it he refers to Highclere as a place that was magnificent for its timber, with the house 'rising church-like from the surrounding woods'. However, he made no analysis of the landscape park, nor the medieval deer park, but confined himself to describing the prehistoric monuments in the region. Thirty years more passed before the archaeological remains within the park were recognised, including the medieval deer park boundary, the fish ponds and areas of ridge and furrow that formerly lay outside the park (Crawford 1953, 194, 202).

THE MEDIEVAL EPISCOPAL LANDSCAPE[1]

The bishops of Winchester had a palace at Highclere consisting of a hall, chamber and chapel, and a series of domestic buildings comprising a kitchen, bakehouse and a dairy; other buildings included a grange and stables. Attached to the episcopal palace was a garden, first recorded in 1218–19 when a *new* garden with 61 fruit trees was planted. It was enclosed by a palisade and ditch, and entered through an adjacent court-yard. Within the garden were fruit trees, vege-tables and herbs. The garden was productive throughout the medieval period; in the mid 13th century, for example, cider apples were grown as well as cabbages, beans and other vegetables. There was periodic modification and expansion, as in 1268 when 70 perches (about 352 m) of palisade was erected around the garden. A herb garden is also mentioned in 1286–7, enclosed by a palisade 6 perches long (about 30 m).

In 1368–9 the garden was abandoned and included within the deer park but another gar-den was soon laid out, during Bishop Wyke-ham's work on the manorial buildings in 1375–6, probably in an area which was a for-mer building since rubble had to be cleared to make way. This garden was separated from the park by a ditch, crossed by a bridge.

Highclere was the northernmost of thirteen deer parks held by the bishops of Winchester in Hampshire (Roberts 1988, 68). It was al-ready established by the 12th century when it comprised 10 virgates (about 120 ha) of former arable land. During the next 300 years, like the residence and garden, the park was modified and extended on a number of occasions. In the mid 13th century, for example, there are ref-erences to the new park and in 1308 the park was expanded by nearly 50 acres (22 ha) over an area of eight tenants' holdings. The park was again enlarged in the later 14th century as part of Bishop Wykeham's improvements,

when nearly 2 miles (3 km) were dug around an extension, saplings planted and a hedge laid. In the 15th century it was again extended, this time to the east, taking in arable land from the neigh-bouring vill of Burghclere. The final area of the deer park has been estimated at between 300 and 500 acres (125–208 ha), although the latter fig-ure seems more realistic (Roberts 1994, 230).

Other features in the deer park included a lodge, a rabbit warren and fish ponds; all usual elements of the medieval parkland repertoire. The fishponds, probably situated in the area of Milford Lake are first mentioned in 1309–10; new fishponds were made five years later and by 1370 there were five ponds enclosed by a ditch, 2 furlongs (about 400m) long.

Documents further record that industrial activity, in the form of tile, lime and brick production, also occurred in the park at High-clere from at least the mid 13th century. Tiles, in particular, were produced in considerable numbers. In 1307 production totalled 28,200 and by 1341 this had risen to 58,400. In 1482 there were nine kilns working at Highclere (Dunlop 1940, 71).

THE LANDSCAPE PARK AND GARDENS

The earliest recognisable elements of pleasure gardens at Highclere belong to the later 17th and early 18th centuries when the estate was in the ownership of Robert Herbert. Herbert had suc-ceeded Sir Robert Sawyer in 1692. Sawyer, who was an Attorney General, was responsible for

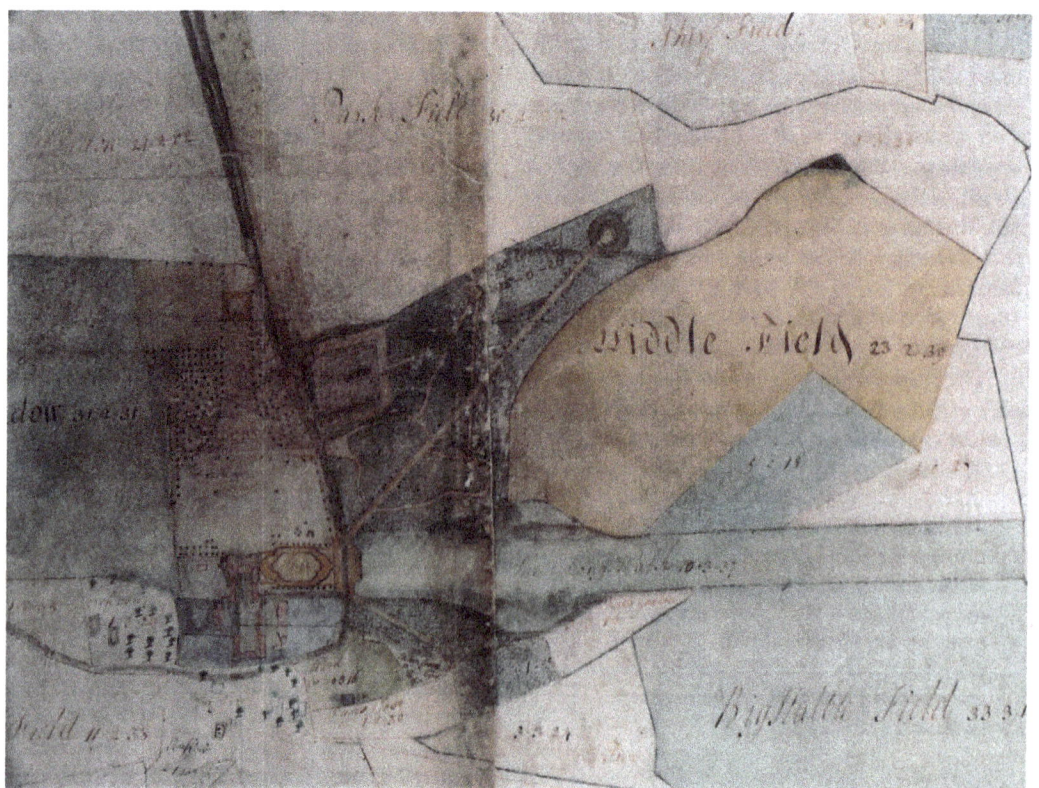

Figure 3
Highclere Castle: an extract from a mid 18th-century plan, showing the garden and part of the park (by kind permission of Hampshire Record Office: HRO 52M88/1).

Figure 4
The earthwork survey north of Highclere Castle. The letters on the plan are explained in the text (RCHME, © Crown copyright).

building a new church in 1689, the ruins of which lie to the north of the present house. The house, which had been rebuilt in 1616, was approached along an avenue from the east (HRO 3M49/23b) while in the south was a large parterre and beyond, a long walk leading towards Sidown Hill. This tree-lined walk clearly pre-dates Herbert's tenure since it is mentioned in Sawyer's will (HCA Box MM A1) and it is therefore likely that the formal garden was initially laid out by Sawyer. On the eastern side there was a lawn and garden with further avenues and serpentine walks. A walled pleasure garden stood to the south east of the house. The picture provided by a mid 18th-century plan is that of a once highly formal layout with long avenues striking out into the surrounding land (HRO 52M88/1), which probably had its origins after the Restoration (Fig 3).

One of Robert Herbert's principal contributions was the construction of several buildings in the park which together have been described as the finest features of a rococo park remaining in Hampshire (Bilikowski 1983, 17). They include Jackdaws Castle, a roofless classical temple erected before 1743 (ibid) and situated on an earthen platform to the east of the house, forming an axial eyecatcher across the lawn. Near the summit of Sidown Hill, clearly visible from the house, was erected a triple-arched folly known as Heavens Gate. Earthworks behind this folly mark the probable site of the little tea rooms mentioned by the Reverend Milles, curate of Highclere, during a visit (ibid). Heavens Gate was approached from the house along a formal avenue of beeches, nearly half a mile long. A rotunda, built about 1760, stands above Dunesmere Lake and is modelled on the Temple of Sibyl at Tivoli (Thacker 1994, 186). It was later modified by Sir Charles Barry, the architect of the present house (Pevsner and Lloyd 1967, 291). Milford Lake House, also designed by Barry, was a summer house or fishing pavilion (ibid).

In 1769 Henry Herbert, later 1st Lord Carnarvon, inherited Highclere from his uncle and soon began to 'improve' his property, transforming the pleasure grounds into a landscape park. He commissioned Capability Brown as designer but the actual works were carried out by estate men under his own supervision. Brown's first visit was followed by a longer one from John Spyers, who between 7 and 25 November 1770, made a full survey of the house and grounds. Brown based his drawings on these surveys (Stroud 1975, 160) and his account book mentions:

> *a general plan for the grounds* [and] *many plans for the alterations of the house and offices – a great deal of trouble to me* [and] *a separate plan for the intended water and alterations around it.*

The cost of his work amounted to £157 10s (RHS 994.5, 91). Henry Herbert was also responsible for planting hundreds of trees in the park, including many cedars, planted either in clumps, individually, or in belts. Around some of the clumps are circular embanked enclosures. Existing stands were modified as another important element of the landscape. A deep cutting through the earlier formal parterre on the south side of the house was probably made at this time in order to improve the view towards the bottom of Sidown Hill (Fig 4). Water was an integral feature in this new landscape. In the mid 18th century there were three large rectangular ponds (HRO 91 M70/PZ9) which were amalgamated to form Milford Lake. Dunesmere Lake was created by damming a stream and is possibly the 'intended water' referred to in Brown's account book.

THE EARTHWORK SURVEY AND FIELD INVESTIGATION

The RCHME survey north and east of Highclere house revealed a very complex relict landscape (Fig 4: a–q). The earliest surviving features are part of a prehistoric field system which can be seen as a regular alignment of slight banks and lynchets, often appearing to influence the layout of subsequent features (Fig 4: a). The boundary banks of the fields are on average 8–10 m wide, while the lynchets average about 0.4 m high. To the south of Highclere Castle, in the woodland leading to Sidown Hill, further prehistoric field lynchets are evident.

Overlying this early field system, and incorporating many of its elements, is a complicated weave of medieval ridge and furrow cultivation, no doubt from fields worked by tenants of the bishop. Whether or not these fields were extinguished by the deer park is not clear on the ground.

Much of the course of the medieval deer park boundary can still be traced (Fig 5), defined by a prominent bank with an external ditch. Its course partly reflects the line of a parish boundary, a common occurrence in many deer parks. In places along the eastern side, the boundary has a double bank and ditch suggesting possible modification or maintenance. To the north of Highclere Castle, a bank (Fig 4: k–l) flanked intermittently by a shallow ditch, marks the course of the deer park boundary. This feature, which clearly overlies a number of elements of the field system, continues north beyond the modern road. It can also be traced slightly to the south of Jackdaws Castle extending in an easterly direction (Fig 5). A possible earlier boundary can be seen as a very low linear bank with a ditch on either side. This feature extends in an east–west direction some 350 m from Tile Pits Coppice (Fig 5).

There are also earthworks which possibly mark former settlement sites. Approximately 400 m to the north of Highclere Castle, occupying land on either side of the modern road, is a complex of sub-rectangular earthworks extending in an east–west direction (Fig 4). Those to the south of the road are better preserved and distinguishable as shallow depressions measuring about 10 m by 5 m. They are bordered on the north by a hollow way (Fig 4: b–c) and on the south by a terrace (Fig 4: d–e). To the south of this complex is a well-defined track (Fig 4: f–g), along which are at least two further smaller concentrations of earthworks, one with potential structures and recessed building platforms (Fig 4: h), the other immediately west of the point marked (g). Some 150 m to the south of this point, yet another group contains at least six sub-rectangular hollows and platforms (Fig 4: j), some of which are depicted on a map of 1743 (HRO 52 M88/1). Finally, on the lawn between the house and Jackdaws Castle, and to the north of the house, are a series of very shallow earthworks including rectangular enclosures and two circular banked enclosures (Fig 4: n).

Throughout the southern part of the park there are occasional clay and chalk pits (for example that marked as (m) on Figure 4 and the area of the pond). Clay was also probably dug just beyond the eastern park boundary at some time since the profile here is much wider and deeper than elsewhere with a further area of quarrying slightly to the east.

On the southern side of the house is part of the former Long Walk which has been destroyed by a large sunken feature (Fig 4: p). Finally, describing an arc approximately 100 m in front of the house along a fence-line, and truncating the former deer park boundary, is an undated ha-ha (Fig 4: q) which continues beyond Jackdaws Castle. On the northern side it is still extant, whilst to the east the ditch has been infilled.

DISCUSSION

Although Highclere is justly renowned for its park and gardens, it is worth reflecting that this is a landscape that has been created only during the past 250 years, a short time in the overall history of the area. Preserved within it are the remains of older landuse patterns which are of equal importance.

Whilst the archaeological remains suggest extensive prehistoric agriculture, Highclere enters history in the 8th century when the Saxon king, Cuthred, granted land at Clere to Winchester. The grant included Highclere (Crawford 1922, 75; Sawyer 1968, S258). The likelihood of a pre-Conquest settlement is therefore strong and is supported by the recovery of Saxo-Norman pottery within what may have been an enclosure[2], slightly to the north of the point marked (g) on

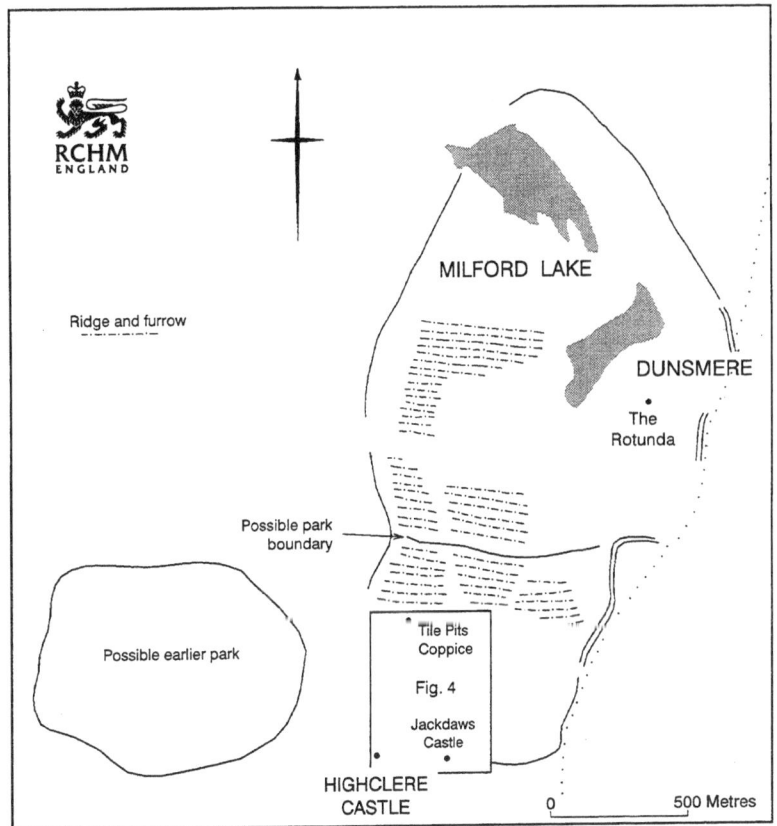

Figure 4. Further north the survey recorded a number of rectangular pits, which morphologically could be interpreted as settlement earthworks, although excavation produced only broken tiles set on compacted chalk floors. This area was known as Tile Pits Coppice in the mid 18th century, thus reflecting a former landuse (HRO 91M70/PZ9). Nevertheless, it is plausible that a settlement existed here, perhaps dating to the 10th or 11th century, which moved following the creation or expansion of the deer park.

The bishops of Winchester had a palace at Highclere from at least the early 13th century, possibly sited near the present Highclere Castle (Upcott 1911, 285; Hughes 1994, 211), which occupies relatively high ground with the deer park extending to the north. An undated engraving, probably of 18th-century date, shows that before alteration, Highclere Castle may have incorporated two phases; one side has crenellations and stair towers of a style normally associated with the late medieval period, whilst a second side has gables of Jacobean style (HRO Top 160/2/8/L). A geophysical survey in the area north and east of the house also suggests that the remains of two courtyards lie buried here.

However, some consideration should be given to the possibility that the episcopal palace was not on the site of the present house. There was extensive building work in the mid 13th century and also during the episcopacy of Wykeham in the later 14th century, when a new garden was laid out over an area of building rubble. The

Figure 5
The medieval deer park boundaries at Highclere (RCHME, © Crown copyright).

finding of Saxo-Norman pottery within a possible enclosure to the north of the house and the earthwork evidence for several settlement foci suggests a more complex settlement pattern.

From the 12th century the deer park lay to the north of the bishop's garden and throughout the medieval period it was constantly being maintained and enlarged. One of these earlier boundaries extends east–west a few hundred metres to the north of Tile Pits Coppice (Fig 5). This may date to the late 14th century since, in 1370, the deer park was extended which required the construction of 3 km of paling (the actual boundary distance to the north from this point is 3.2 km). The park was also later enlarged to the east taking in former arable land. In the northern part of the park there are a number of wood-banks forming enclosures, which may reflect earlier woodland management.

The deer park boundary has an external ditch along part of its perimeter; this is contrary to what one might expect to find in a deer park since the ditch is usually internal, thus giving the deer a greater obstacle to clear. However, excavation across the park boundary to the north of the pond confirmed that there was in fact an internal ditch measuring 1 m deep and 3 m across at the top. The apparent absence of an internal ditch along part of the perimeter may suggest a later modification or adaptation of the park.

To the west of the deer park is a large circular enclosure of some 8 hectares bounded on the south side by a hollow way. This enclosure may be a detached park, or possibly an earlier park (Fig 5).

Throughout much of the southern part of the park there is evidence of arable cultivation in the form of ridge and furrow. The earthworks of this ploughing are slight and it is probable that it is a relic of a short-term ploughing episode which took place either before the area was emparked, or during the post-medieval period.

CONCLUSION

The archaeological investigation of the High-clere estate has led to the recognition of a landscape of national importance, not only for the more recent pleasure grounds and landscape park, which were largely understood from estate maps and documentation, but also for the identification of the prehistoric field system and medieval landscape. The earthwork survey, coupled with other archaeological techniques, has enabled us to identify the complexity of the medieval landscape. Underlying all these features is the extensive prehistoric field system which has survived despite the later adaptations. When examining parkland landscapes elsewhere in the country we should continually be aware of the possibility that features of earlier landuse survive.

NOTES

1 Much of the information, unless otherwise stated, comes from the Bishop of Winchester's Pipe Rolls as they pertain to Highclere. The pipe rolls were transcribed by Dr C Phillpotts for Hampshire County Council.
2 The excavation and geophysical surveys were carried out by H Stevens of Southampton University. I am grateful to him for discussing the results of his work with me in advance of his PhD dissertation.

ACKNOWLEDGEMENTS

I would like to express my gratitude to colleagues at the RCHME, particularly David McOmish and David Field, who carried out much of the survey at Highclere, and to Deborah Cunliffe who prepared the drawings for publication. The documentary research was undertaken by Dr C Phillpotts on behalf of Hampshire County Council. H Stevens from Southampton University discussed the results of his excavations and geophysical surveys in advance of his PhD thesis. I would also like to thank D Hopkins of Hampshire County Council for allowing me access to material relating to Highclere and to J Thorpe, the archivist at Highclere Castle, who made available the material held there. Finally I would like to thank The Rt Hon the Earl of Carnarvon, without whose permission and interest in our work none of this would have been possible.

The archived plans and site accounts are available for public consultation during normal office hours at the National Monuments Record Centre, Great Western Village, Kemble Drive, Swindon SN2 2GZ; telephone (01793) 414600, fax (01793) 414606.

LANDSCAPE WITH GARDENS: AERIAL, TOPOGRAPHICAL AND GEOPHYSICAL SURVEY AT HAMSTEAD MARSHALL, BERKSHIRE

Graham D Keevill and Neil Linford

ABSTRACT

This paper describes archaeological fieldwork undertaken on a late 17th-century formal garden at Hamstead Marshall, near Newbury, Berkshire. The history of the site is outlined briefly, especially the post-medieval elements which provide an essential background to the archaeological remains. These are also described, while the results of archaeological research to date are presented in some detail. Some thoughts are presented on the potential for further archaeological work on the site.

It is also our purpose to demonstrate the potential and complementary uses of three quite distinct archaeological survey techniques in the assessment and analysis of historic landscapes, including gardens: topographical (or earthwork), aerial and geophysical surveys. We do not seek to establish the uniqueness of garden archaeology, but rather to emphasise its commonality with other areas of landscape archaeology.

HAMSTEAD MARSHALL

Hamstead Marshall is a small parish on the Berkshire Downs a few miles to the west of Newbury. The present village comprises a dispersed scatter of houses and cottages, spread from the bottom to the top of the Kennet Valley. Geologically the site is dominated by clay on the valley sides with a gravel cap on the plateau, while the river and canal run side-by-side in the valley bottom to the north of the main part of the settlement. The immediate area is rich in archaeology. Recent work has established a strong Mesolithic presence in the valley bottom (Reynier 1994), while a Roman kiln site was excavated some years ago in advance of gravel extraction from the uplands on the south side of the valley. The subject of this paper, however, is the remarkable medieval and post-medieval landscape which survives around

St Mary's Church (Figs 6 and 7), itself probably of 12th-century origin (Bonney and Dunn 1989).

Historical summary

The medieval history of Hamstead Marshall has been dealt with in some detail in the Victoria County History (VCH 1906), while the use of the site by Edward III is dealt with elsewhere (Colvin 1963, 242–4). Bonney and Dunn (1989) provide a useful summary, while Stokes (1996) paints a lively picture of events. It will be sufficient here to record that the village appears in the Domesday survey, but with *'nothing to distinguish it from its neighbours'* (Bonney and Dunn 1989, 175); its later medieval history is dominated by the Marshal family, powerful movers on the national scene, and the royal connection already noted.

The post-medieval occupation of the site, though short-lived (but see Stokes 1996, 45), is the main focus of this paper. A grand new house surrounded by formal gardens and landscaped grounds was built by the Earl of Craven in the 17th century, on land formerly occupied in part by the medieval village, which was removed to make way for the new house. Fortunately, the contemporary fashion for commissioning depictions of country houses was followed at Hamstead, with the result that Johannes Kip has provided us with a detailed panoramic view of the site around 1700 as the starting-point for any study of the post-medieval landscape (Fig 6). Our good fortune is redoubled by the fact that the house was destroyed by fire in 1718, although Stokes has suggested (1996, 45) that part of the building continued to be used.

A brief description of the landscape depicted by Kip is worthwhile at this point. Firstly, of course there is the fine house itself, evidently built on a U-shaped ground-plan. The house has three storeys and an attic, with an imposing

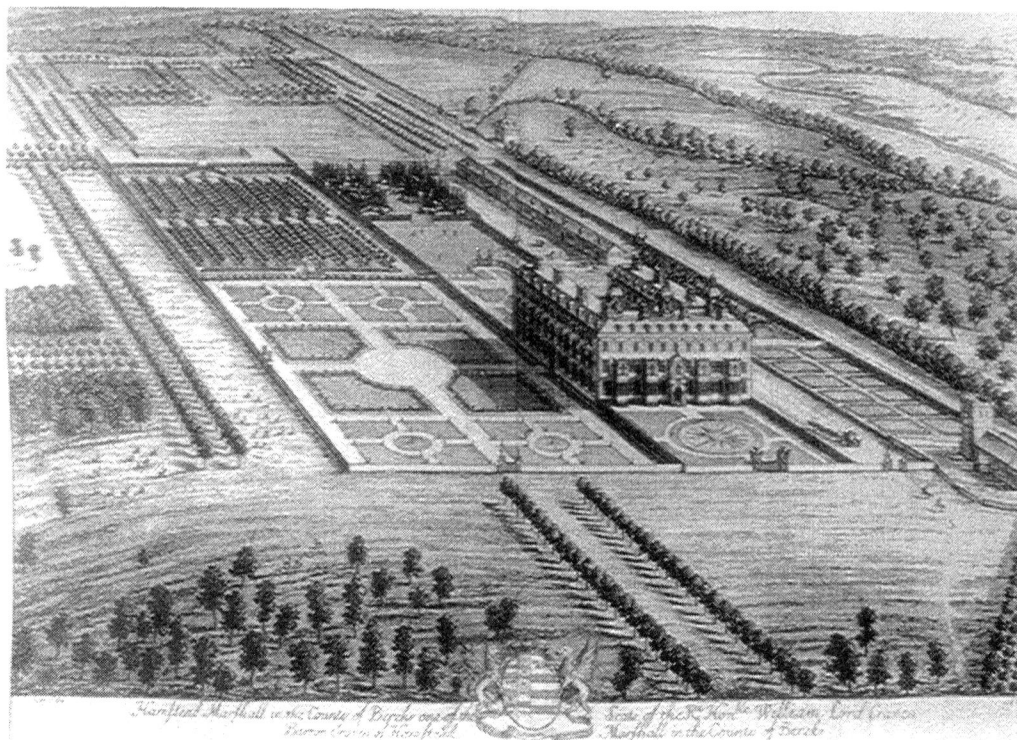

Figure 6
Johannes Kip's engraving of the Earl of Craven's new house at Hamstead Marshall, c 1700 (Knyff and Kip 1707).

eastern façade boasting a grand entrance with paired flanking bays, each of which rises to first-floor level. The surrounding landscape is carefully arranged with a central core of formal parterres to the south and east of the house and other gardens contained within high walls, interrupted at intervals by grand, paired columns. St Mary's Church can be seen clearly, close to the house and this central ensemble is surrounded by a planted park of avenues and geometrical arrangements of trees.

There is a fascinating hint of the landscaping policy in John Aubrey's *Monumenta Britannica* (Fowles 1982, 682–3). Following a description of Silbury Hill, Wiltshire, Aubrey goes on to record that:

By Hampstead Marshall Park in Berkshire (a seat of the Earl of Craven) is a hill like Silbury Hill (by the name .... [no name is given]) on which Captain William Winde designs to make a screw-walk, as at the keep of the Castle of Marlborough, at the Lord Seymour's.

He continues:

Memorandum the Roman mount at Hampstead Marshall (near Newbury) which the Captain W Wynd hath now converted into a screw walk, like the keep of the castle at Marlborough, and is almost as high as that, with a deep graff [ditch] about it. And Captain Wynd farther tells me that there is a hill called Castle Hill near/within half a mile of Hamstead Marshall, greater than that before mentioned; and there is also another mount near, but not so great (ibid 684).

Screw walks such as this were scarcely a new development. One had been built in Henry VIII's Privy Garden at Hampton Court (Jacques 1995, 23–5, fig 34).

Archaeological summary

As the history suggests, the landscape of Hamstead Marshall is a complex one, with extensive earthworks relating to several successive phases of landuse. The archaeological landscape (Figs 7 and 8) comprises: a pair of adjacent motte-and-bailey castles (Bonney and Dunn 1989, fig 2) with a third enigmatic but apparently incomplete motte (Bonney and Dunn 1989, fig 3) at some distance to the east; the insubstantial earthworks of a deserted medieval village (the original Hamstead Marshall, clustered to the east of the church and removed to make way for Craven's house and grounds); an extensive park pale encompassing an area of approximately 101 hectares; fishponds; St Mary's Church itself and its graveyard; and most importantly in the context of this paper, traces of the post-medieval house and its formal gardens. The earthworks are generally in good condition, with the principal remains (the motte-and-baileys and the pale) seeming to be especially well preserved. At the moment, however, it is difficult to discern the extent to which the monuments have been affected by post-medieval work associated with the landscaping around the new house.

Presumably we can take Aubrey's reference at face value; therefore at least one of the mottes must have suffered extensive changes at the hands of Sir William Wynd. It is by no means clear which of the three mottes he took in hand.

14

The mound with the *'deep graff about it'* probably refers to the western motte, with the eastern one being the other *'mount near, but not so great'*. Against this, perhaps, is the fact that the eastern motte is so clearly in poorer condition than the western one. Wynd's Castle Hill surely equates to the incomplete earthwork in the park to the east, or castle 1 (using the numbering system proposed by Myers 1932), although the formation of the earthwork is admittedly reminiscent of the screw walk.

As for the post-medieval landscape, only a small proportion of the scene depicted by Kip survives above ground, or so it seems at ground level. The house is the most obvious casualty, not surprisingly given that it suffered such a catastrophic fire; it has long since gone, although there is a pronounced hollow in the field over its approximate position which probably reflects the former presence of cellars. Furthermore, recent ploughing has brought large quantities of brick and tile to the surface. Much of the high boundary wall still exists (though not, crucially, in the area of the parterres), and most of the nine pairs of columns are intact, though the brickwork and especially the stone details are deteriorating. The surviving medieval remains can also be taken as a relict element of the post-medieval landscape (the church, for instance, is clearly used as part of the scheme), though the extent to which they were altered by Craven and his team is unclear. Some of the larger trees in the park are probably original plantations of the late 17th or early 18th century.

Much of the medieval landscape remained unrecognised for what it was until quite recently. Aubrey's description of one mound as 'Roman'

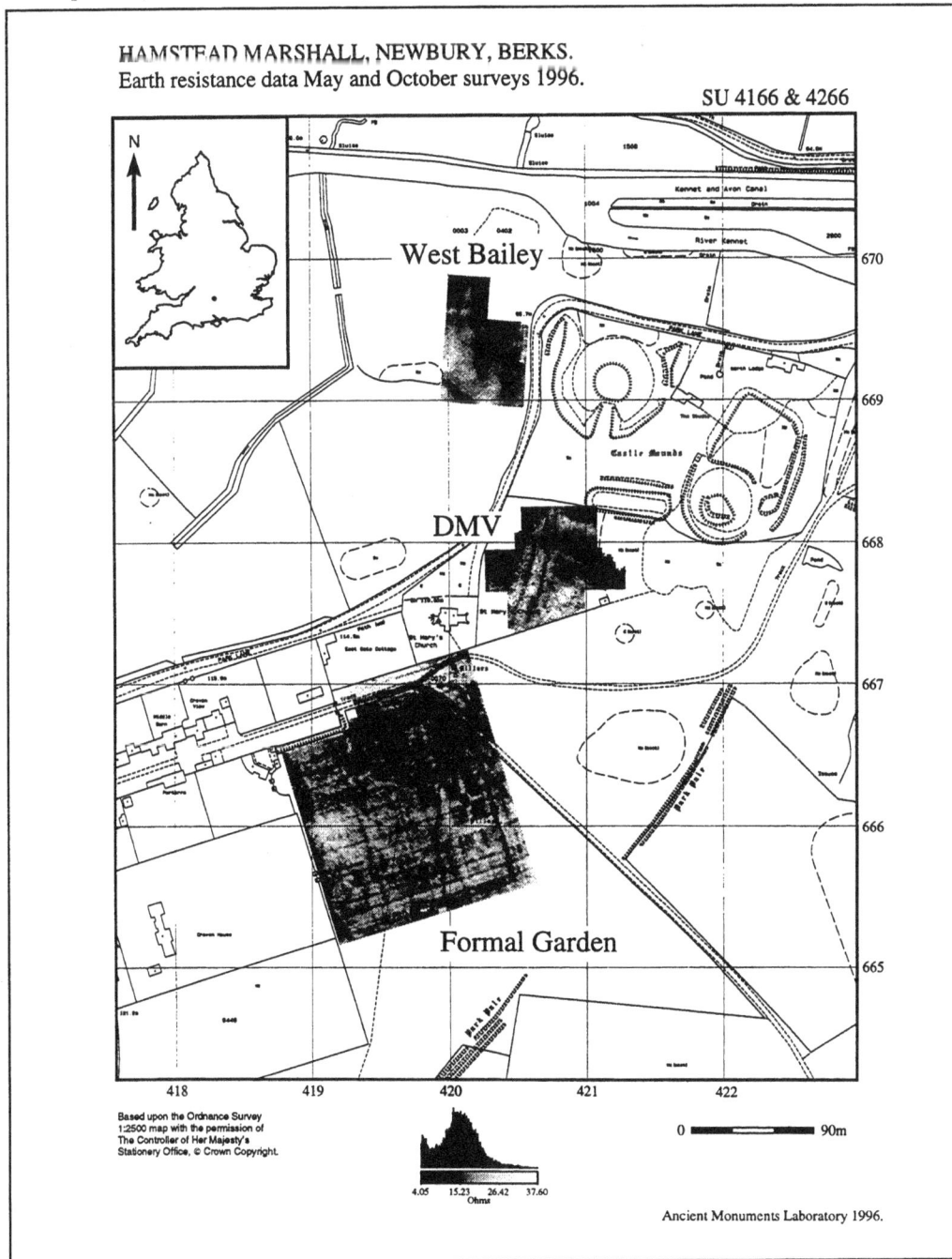

HAMSTEAD MARSHALL, NEWBURY, BERKS.
Earth resistance data May and October surveys 1996.

SU 4166 & 4266

West Bailey

DMV

Formal Garden

Ancient Monuments Laboratory 1996.

Figure 7
Location of the site showing unprocessed resistivity data from the three geophysical survey areas (the west bailey, the deserted medieval village and the formal garden) superimposed on the Ordnance Survey base map (English Heritage, © Crown copyright).

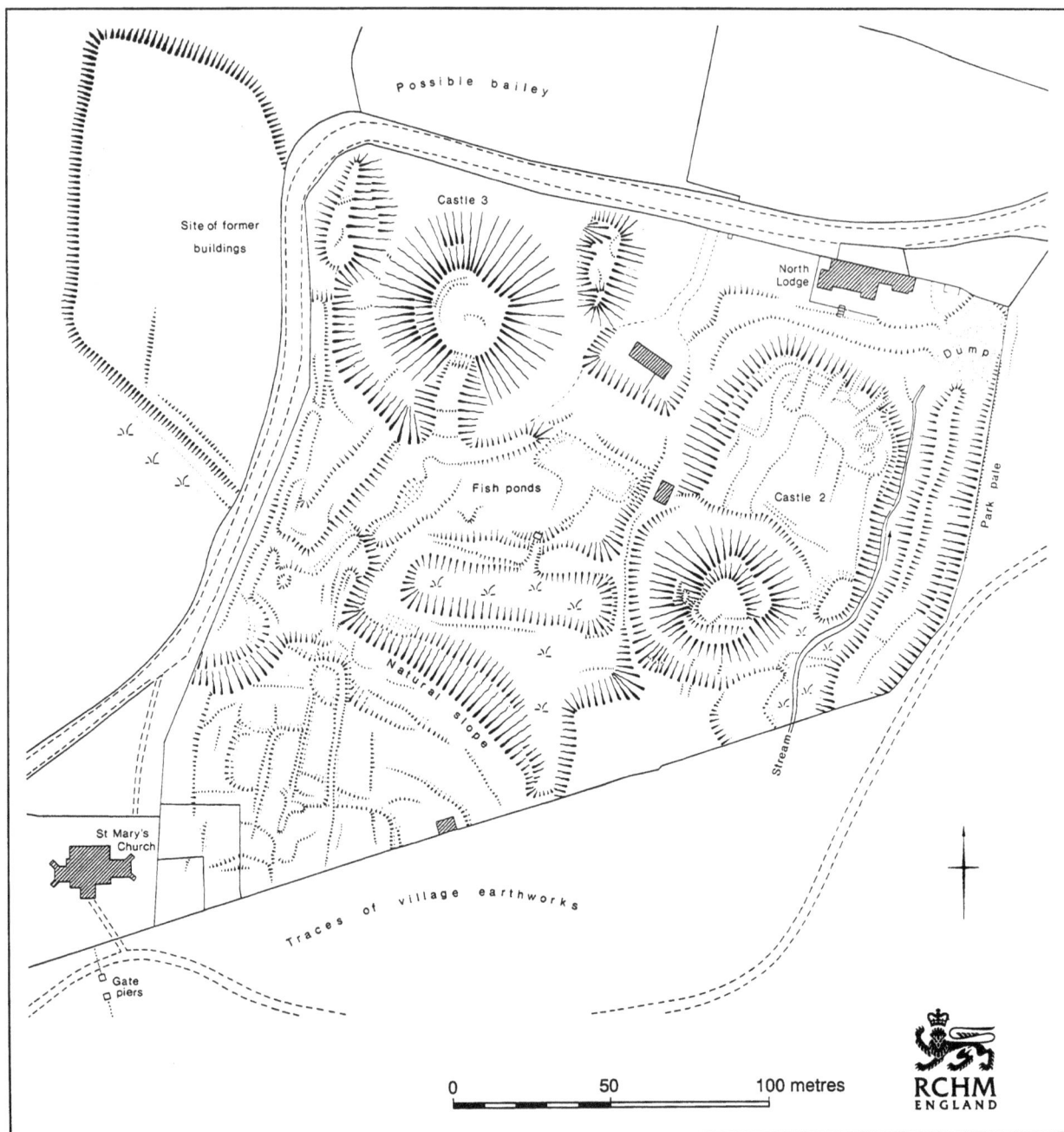

Figure 8
Survey of the principal earthworks at Hamstead Marshall showing the tentative identification of the west bailey platform (RCHME, © Crown copyright).

is notable, especially in the context of its juxta-position and comparison to Silbury Hill in his journal. At the same time, however, he compared Wynd's proposal to Marlborough Castle's keep, and noted Wynd's comments about the nearby Castle Hill. Apparently, Aubrey himself did not visit the site but simply indulged in reportage, and so his mistake is understandable. The error was compounded by others, including the Ordnance Survey (25-inch map, Berkshire XLII, 3) and the Victoria County History, who recorded the mottes as 'tumuli' (VCH 1924, 280). It was left to that great archaeologist J N L Myers to correct these mistakes and make the appropriate ascription to the medieval period (Myers 1932).

Two of the motte-and-bailey earthworks (castles 2 and 3 in Myres 1932), the fishponds and the partial remains of the medieval village, within the grounds of North Lodge and in the field immediately to the south, are protected as a Scheduled Ancient Monument (Berkshire 19010, originally scheduled in 1924 but upgraded and extended in 1992 under the Monuments Protection Programme), together with castle 1 (Berkshire 19011, scheduled in 1992) and the course of the park pale (Berkshire 19012, scheduled in 1992). The garden columns are listed buildings. Perhaps surprisingly, however, the site of the post-medieval house and formal gardens is not scheduled, and therefore does not enjoy protection. This is unfortunate, as the agricultural regime over this part of the site has changed from pasture to arable in the last decade.

16

Figure 9
*Aerial photograph
of the former manor
house site showing
parchmarks related
to the formal garden
(NMR 58/5225
F21, 48; MOD,
© Crown copyright).*

THE ARCHAEOLOGICAL STUDIES

The first archaeological survey of the site was undertaken in the mid 1980s, when the RCHME undertook a detailed topographical study of the remains within the gardens of North Lodge. Dense undergrowth had recently been cleared here by the new owners, Bob and Sue Brown, who have shown an unfailing interest in and enthusiasm for the site. The surveyors produced plans of a typically comprehensive nature (Bonney and Dunn 1989, figs 1–3), and this picked out the detail of most of the medieval site for the first time. It also demonstrated the complexity of the remains very clearly (Fig 8). The survival of fine detail on the mottes-and-baileys and the recognition of the slight earthworks over the deserted village site were notable discoveries. Unfortunately, access could not be gained to other areas, including the post-medieval house and gardens to the south-west.

Meanwhile, however, it became apparent that extraordinary survey data had been collected almost by accident over several decades from the 1940s. Aerial photographs (APs) had been taken in the area for a variety of purposes by various authorities (including the Royal Air Force), but not for archaeological survey. At least two of the sorties covered Hamstead Marshall and the results deserve some exploration. Figure 9, from the late 1950s, clearly shows as parchmarks much of the detailed layout recorded by Kip. The outlines of the main parterres to the south of the

house site are especially visible, with the paired rectangular arrangements of double parterres showing up particularly clearly. The most recent photograph (Fig 13), taken by Sue Brown during the winter of 1996, shows much the same arrangement from an oblique angle. The significance of this remarkable photograph will be returned to below.

THE GEOPHYSICAL SURVEYS

Introduction

Geophysical surveys were undertaken during 1996 by the Ancient Monuments Laboratory. A more complete analysis of the geophysical survey data is available in Linford 1997. The general principles of geophysical surveying and its applicability to garden archaeology have been described elsewhere (Cole *et al* 1997; David 1995).

The geophysical surveys were conducted during three site visits. The first, during May 1996, investigated the west bailey and deserted medieval village sites. This was followed by two further visits in October and November 1996, after the harvest of the forage maize crop, to conduct the surveys over the formal garden.

Trial magnetometer survey over the site of the supposed west bailey building platform proved unsuccessful; thus, earth resistance survey was adopted as the primary investigative technique to examine both this site (Fig 10) and the medieval settlement within the grounds of

17

North Lodge (Fig 11). Following the success of the resistivity technique on other historic garden sites (eg Aspinall and Pocock 1995, Cole *et al* 1997), this technique was also applied to survey the formal garden (Fig 12 A). A subsequent magnetometer scan over this site suggested that the remains of brick wall footings would be revealed magnetically; therefore a detailed survey was conducted over the majority of the area covered by resistivity survey (Fig 12 B) following standard methods (see David 1995).

A Geoscan MPX-15 mutliplexor with an adjustable PA5 electrode frame was used to simultaneously collect 0.5 m and 1 m mobile-probe separation data from the deserted medieval village site. The greater separation of the mobile-probe electrodes forces the applied electric current to penetrate further into the ground and will detect anomalies arising from more deeply buried features (Scollar *et al* 1990, 321–4; Linford 1993). It was hoped that the same system could also be applied during the survey of the formal garden. However, extreme contact resistances caused by the quantity of gravel in the topsoil precluded the use of this equipment in this location.

The western bailey

Time restraints and prioritisation of the survey requirements meant that data collection at the west bailey site was restricted to five 30 m squares of resistivity data collected at a 0.5 m x 1 m sample intervals (Fig 10). An initial trial magnetometer survey covering the bailey ramparts (clearly visible as an earthwork in the field) did not produce an encouraging magnetic response. The only convincing resistance anomaly was the bailey rampart which appeared as an outer high resistance anomaly enclosing a low resistance ditch-type response (Fig 10 B:1). Unfortunately the survey did not extend over the rampart at any

other point and thus it is impossible to determine whether the observed response continues along the entire circuit. Other anomalies within this area were too amorphous for precise archaeological interpretation, although a group of very faint ditch-like anomalies (Fig 10 B:2) did appear to form a series of three rectilinear enclosures, possibly indicative of former buildings.

The deserted medieval village

Two data sets were collected from the supposed deserted medieval village site (Fig 11). These comprised a high resolution (0.5 m x 1 m sample interval) near-surface survey (mobile probe spacing = 0.5 m) and a deeper penetrating (mobile probe spacing = 1 m) set collected at a slightly coarser sample interval (1 m x 1 m).

The most obvious anomalies were two linear responses (Fig 11 B:3 and 4) running north – south across the survey area. These anomalies follow the alignment of hollows between linear ridges identified in the earthwork survey and could represent the course of former trackways. A further linear anomaly (Fig 11 B:5) was also evident following the course of an east–west earthwork.

A linear anomaly (Fig 11 B:6) apparently follows the course of the raised ground recorded on the RCHME plan to the west of the survey area and forms a corner with the linear anomaly (Fig 11 B: 7) to the north. Due to its shallow nature it seems most likely that this is associated with the recent animal enclosures sited in this area of the survey (visible on an AP, NMR 543–403, F22 0095, taken in 1958). Several other ditch-like anomalies are not replicated in the earthwork survey.

Pit-like anomalies (marked as open circles, 8, on Fig 11 B) can be seen at approximately 7 m intervals on a regularly spaced grid pattern. The size and ordered distribution of these anomalies

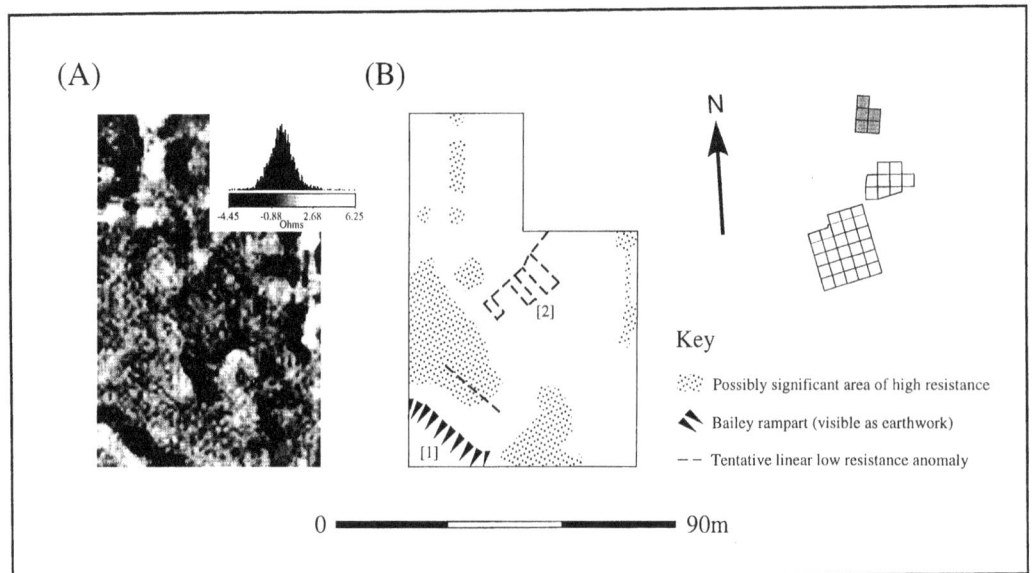

Figure 10
Resistivity data from the west bailey site showing greytone image of enhanced data (A) and summary of significant anomolies (B) (English Heritage, © Crown copyright).

(A)　　　　(B)

-4.45　-0.88　2.68　6.25
Ohms

[2]

[1]

N

Key

░ Possibly significant area of high resistance

◣ Bailey rampart (visible as earthwork)

– – Tentative linear low resistance anomaly

0 ▬▬▬▬▬▬ 90m

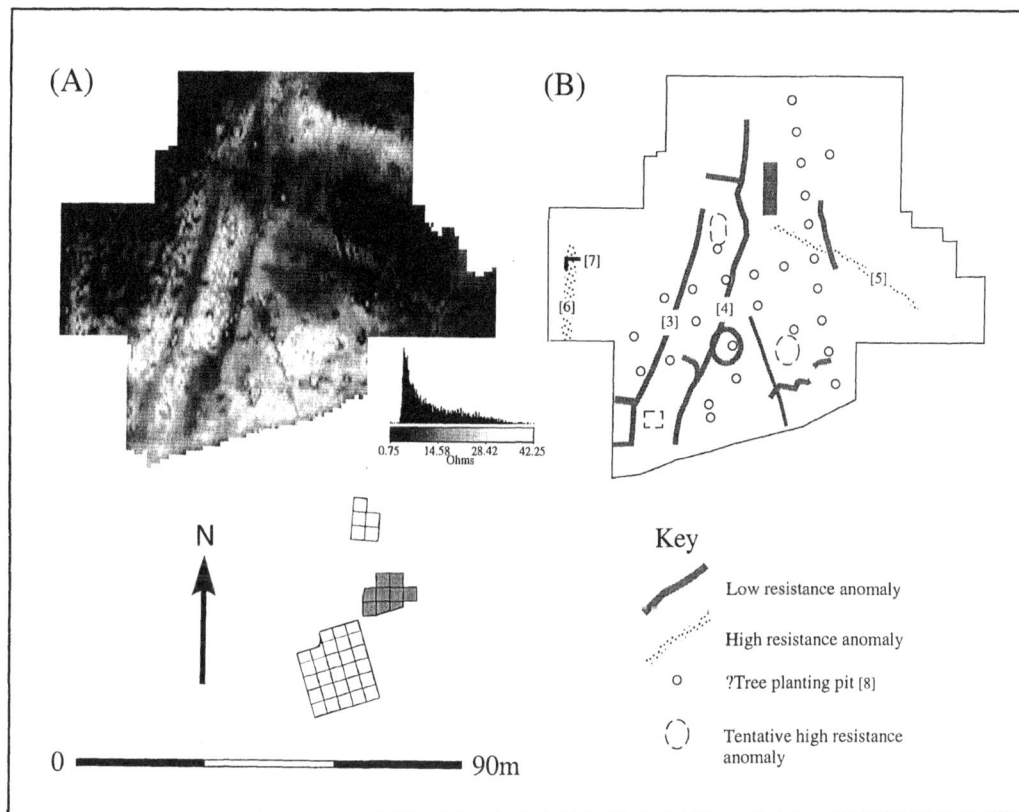

Figure 11
Resistivity data from the deserted medieval village site showing greytone image of enhanced data (A) and summary of significant anomolies (B) (English Heritage, © Crown Copyright).

suggests that they represent former tree planting pits, possibly related to the extensive geometrical layout depicted by the Kip engraving (Fig 6). An alternative explanation may be provided by the occupation of the site by an encampment of United States soldiers towards the end of the Second World War, although the morphology of the anomalies is not suggestive of any recognised military activity from this period (C Dobinson pers comm).

The formal garden

Resistivity survey covered 3 hectares of the formal gardens including the house site (Fig 12). The survey produced a plethora of anomalies, although some of these related to modern features such as the trackway (Fig 12 A:9) from the Home Farm gate piers and the public footpath (Fig 12 A:10). A water trough (Fig 12 C:11) and possibly its pipework (Fig 12 C:12) can also be seen. Linear anomalies (Fig 12 C:13) on a regular east–west alignment, at approximately 10 m intervals, could reflect recent cultivation, field drains, a more ancient agricultural pattern (ridge and furrow?) or perhaps a deliberate attempt to drain or irrigate the site prior to establishing the formal garden design. The absence of any associated anomalies in the magnetic data suggests a lack of ferrous or ceramic material.

More significant archaeological anomalies are evident in the pattern of high resistance linear responses delineating the pathways of the former garden (Fig 12 C:14 and 15) in the south-eastern corner of the survey area. The design comprises four symmetrical parterres each enclosing an approximately 30 m square area separated by paths radiating from a central apparently circular planting bed or lawn. Two of the parterres appear unambiguously within the resistivity data together with the main arterial pathways (Fig 12 C:16–18). Path 18 apparently continues eastwards parallel to the course of the south wall of the garden, though its definition is somewhat obscured by the highly variable background readings over this part of the site. The linear anomalies correspond to parchmarks visible on the APs and they probably derive from compacted gravel walkways between the planting beds or lawns. The beds themselves would be expected to produce low resistance anomalies due to the quantity of moisture-retentive organic matter added to the soil as manure (Cole *et al* 1997). However, the underlying geology of the site combined with recent mechanical agriculture has ploughed an appreciable quantity of gravel (some no doubt from the original garden paths) into the current topsoil thus obscuring the identification of such features.

The course of the garden wall visible on the Kip engraving is also evident in the resistivity data and four convincing lengths (Fig 12 C:19–22) are identifiable. All exhibit linear low resistance anomalies approximately 2 m wide. This is a surprising response for the remains of a wall footing, which ought to produce a high resistance anomaly. The remains of the wall may have been robbed out, or the porous fabric of the bricks may retain more moisture than the surrounding sub-

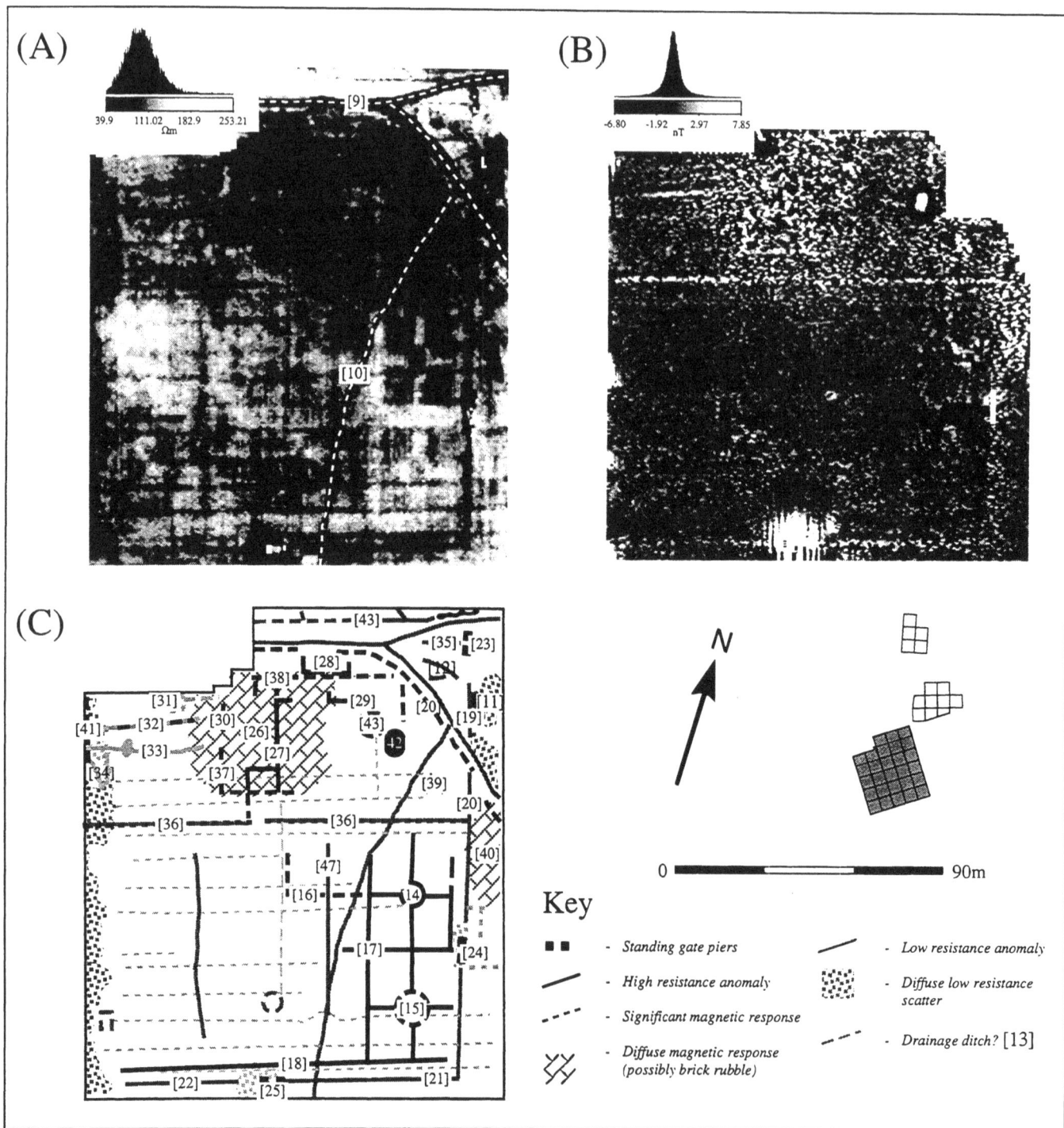

Figure 12
Resistivity data from the formal garden site showing greytone image of enhanced data (A), greytone image of unprocessed magnetometer data (B) and summary of significant anomolies (C) (English Heritage, © Crown copyright).

soil. A similar low resistance response is evident around each of the isolated gate piers (Fig 12 C:23–25).

Another area of very low resistance (Fig 12 C:26) was found over the hollow marking the site of the former mansion house, coinciding with a diffuse area of magnetic disturbance (Fig 12 B). An area of low resistance within the depression might be expected but the anomaly extends beyond this and is apparently bounded by a group of linear high resistance anomalies (Fig 12 C:27–30). It seems most likely that these anomalies represent the remains of the house's wall footings.

A series of linear low resistance anomalies (Fig 12 C:31–34) to the west of the house may represent drainage conduits. This would concur with the remains of a vaulted brick conduit at the edge of the arable field against the boundary wall of Craven House. Additional anecdotal evidence (J Homes pers comm) suggests that other conduits exist to the north of the former manor house, while another conduit was exposed recently in the grounds of North Lodge (S Brown pers comm). The course of anomaly 35 passes through a pair of standing gate piers (Fig 12 C:23) although there is little evidence to suggest that it continues beyond the garden.

An initial magnetometer scan over the course of the former east garden wall suggested that the brick footings would produce an identifiable magnetic response. Full magnetometer survey confirmed this and has identified a number of apparently brick structures. The magnetic response of a brick structure is relatively diagnostic as fired clay is generally rich in ferro/ferri magnetic minerals, producing a strong induced magnetisation in the earth's ambient magnetic field. More importantly, as each brick cools in the kiln after firing the magnetic material within the clay will acquire a thermoremanent magnetisation causing each brick to retain a relatively strong permanent magnetic moment (Bevan 1994). Magnetic surveys over brick foundations confirm the relatively intense yet erratic nature of such features (Linford forthcoming) and many brick-like anomalies are evident within the formal garden.

The garden wall appears as a brick-like magnetic response corresponding to resistance anomalies 20–22. A strong linear response, (Fig 12 C:36), bisects the garden site and corresponds with a low resistance anomaly. The latter lies directly south of the house site, represented in the magnetic data as a diffuse area of disturbance (Fig 12 C:26) containing brick-like linear responses (Fig 12 C:37 and 38). The magnetic disturbance in this area is doubtless caused by a scatter of brick rubble within the soil and the underlying wall footings of the house. Similar areas of disturbance lie to the east of the manor house (Fig 12 C:39) and beyond the garden wall (Fig 12 C:40). These could represent former brick-built structures. Anomaly 40 may be related to rubble from the garden wall although it is difficult to explain the concentration of rubble here compared to the other lengths of the dismantled wall.

Immediately west of the house, low resistance anomaly 32 correlates with a strong positive response in the magnetic data suggestive of a ferrous or ceramic pipe/brick-conduit possibly joining a ferrous pipe (Fig 12 C:41). The area immediately to the east of the house is dominated by an intense (~150nT) magnetic response (Fig 12 C:42); unfortunately it is impossible to determine from the magnetic response alone whether 42 is related to a feature of the original garden or to a more recent burial of ferrous detritus. A negative anomaly, (Fig 12 C:43), close to 42, could be a circular gravel path from the original garden.

Additional elements of the original garden design are replicated as magnetic anomalies over the site of the former parterres (14 and 15) identified by the resistivity survey. The magnetic response is most apparent over the east pathway of 14 which produces a negative anomaly bounded to the north by positive readings possibly indicative of surviving brick cutwork separating the original gravel path from the adjoining planting bed. Other magnetic anomalies here are less distinct, although the location of the former parterres can be distinguished from the more uniform response of the gravel paths (17 and 18).

COMPARISON OF THE SURVEYS

It is of interest to compare the results of the geophysical survey with the extremely clear AP evidence gathered thirty years ago (Fig 9), before the Craven estate was sold and the site of the former garden reverted to arable land. The parchmark patterns are most readily comparable to the earth resistance data as both techniques rely on a contrast in soil moisture to develop a distinguishable anomaly. In the case of the AP evidence three of the parterre designs and attendant pathways can be identified, the clearest corresponding to anomaly 14, while the other two in the south-west corner of the site have not been detected by the geophysical survey. The enclosing wall of the garden does not appear as a parchmark on the APs, an observation consistent with the results of the resistivity survey which suggest that the brick foundations are more moisture retentive than the high resistance gravel subsoil. The quality of the APs is reduced in the northern part of the survey area and only a single raised mound (now apparently ploughed out) is visible; this may be related to the former house.

Comparison of both the AP and the geophysical evidence with the Kip engraving confirms the basic integrity of the latter. The carriage drive is of interest as it corresponds to the area of extremely high resistivity recorded to the north of the formal garden site. It is possible that the high background resistance in this area is a direct result of a deliberately compacted layer of gravel laid to assist the passage of horse-drawn traffic visiting the house. The Kip engraving also shows a regular alignment of trees apparently extending north east of St Mary's Church. The exact location of this cannot be ascertained from Kip's artificially elevated angle, but the tree planting apparently extended to the north of the church and may well explain the regular pattern of low resistance anomalies observed during the survey of this area (Fig 11).

Immediately after the magnetometer survey was conducted in November 1996 Sue Brown obtained an extremely clear AP of the formal garden site (Fig 13). It is unclear whether this image represents a soilmark, presumably indicating accumulations of gravel in the topsoil, or the differential thawing of the heavy frost that covered the site at the time that the photograph was taken. In either case the photograph reveals a pattern of pathways corroborating the parterre garden to the south of the manor house, as depicted by the Kip engraving. In particular, this photograph shows details of the geometric designs in the south west corner of the garden that

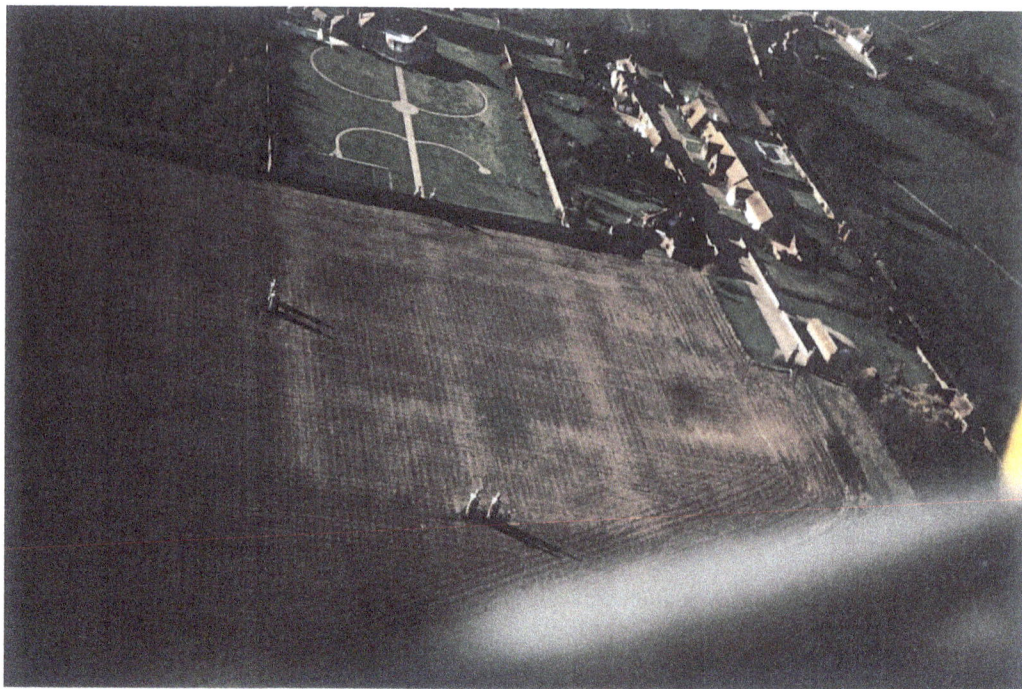

Figure 13
Aerial view of the former garden at Hamstead Marshall in 1996, showing as a soil or frost mark (by kind permission of Sue Brown).

have not been reproduced in the geophysical survey data. Furthermore, many of the linear anomalies in the photograph appear to be alternately displaced along their length in an east–west orientation. This would suggest that the material causing the patterns is susceptible to damage from the modern ploughing regime and exists predominantly in the very near-surface topsoil.

CONCLUSION

Kip's illustration of the post-medieval house and gardens at Hamstead Marshall remains as the starting point for studying this period of the site's history. Much of the archaeological work to date has been invaluable in confirming the essential accuracy of specific elements he depicted, especially in the gardens. It is important to recognise, however, that the archaeological data are fully interpretable in their own right: elements such as the parterres and garden walls are so clear as to need no external source comparison. Equally, the surveys have presented new information – for example with regard to water management – which cannot be gleaned from Kip.

The surveys also provide critical material for comparing the *condition* of the site at various times. The APs and geophysical results suggest that the gardens and house have suffered degradation since ploughing was introduced about a

decade ago: scarcely surprising, but it is essential to know and understand this if the future management of the site is to look to its long-term preservation. In particular, is there enough of the house and garden surviving to warrant an extension of the existing Scheduled Ancient Monument (Berkshire no 19010, currently covering North Lodge) to encompass some or all of the survey area? Equally, is there enough left to allow any potential for reconstruction?

As for the future, determination of these issues will only be possible if further fieldwork goes ahead. Extension of the topographical survey to cover previously inaccessible areas is essential, although cultivation may have reduced the potential for recording earthworks much beyond the hollow of the house. Sue Brown's work shows that further APs, taken in the right conditions, would be invaluable for comparative purposes. Ultimately, however, further archaeological study of the site is likely to require some excavation as this still offers the best way of establishing the condition of the archaeology within and under the plough horizon. This is all the more important because the post-medieval gardens at Hamstead Marshall seem to be of a single short-lived phase, with little, if any, reworking by subsequent gardeners. Ultimately, geophysical surveys may help us to see beneath the soil, but they will not help us to lift it.

THE CONSCIOUS CONVERSION OF EARLIER EARTHWORKS IN THE DESIGN OF PARKS AND GARDENS

Mark Bowden

ABSTRACT

No English park or garden was ever laid out in virgin territory. Garden designers have always made use of topographical features and this opportunism has often extended to prominent man-made features from former landscapes. Some pre-existing landscape features, such as the earthwork remains of cleared villages, may have survived despite emparkment but others were deliberately incorporated in park or garden designs and have therefore survived because of emparkment. The starting point for this paper is a group of examples from North Yorkshire but the syndrome is found much more widely.

TEMPLE GROUNDS, RICHMOND

Culloden Tower in Temple Grounds at Richmond, North Yorkshire, built in a flamboyant mix of rococo and gothick styles, was almost certainly designed by Daniel Garrett (Hatcher 1990, 218), a close associate of Lord Burlington and William Kent (Leach 1974). Temple Grounds were the gardens associated with Yorke House, home of the Yorke family, which stood at the west end of Bargate Green; Yorke House was demolished in the 1820s. The Yorkes were a prominent local Whig family who celebrated the final defeat of the Jacobites and the securing of the Protestant succession in 1746 by the building of this tower. According to Clarkson (1821, 328), however, it was built upon the ruins of a pre-existing medieval fortification – of the type usually called a pele-tower – known as Hudswell Tower. This is a clear example of the deliberate reuse of an earlier architectural feature in a garden (though recent research has found no supporting evidence for Clarkson's statement (Valerie Hepworth pers comm)).

However, my subject is the deliberate reuse or conversion of less obvious archaeological features in the design of ornamental parks. Again

Temple Grounds at Richmond provide us with an example, albeit a somewhat unusual one, involving industrial archaeology: the Yorkes constructed a river walk along the banks of the Swale, with grottoes built into the adit portals of a series of failed copper mines. (Interestingly, the more successful copper mines in Billy Bank Wood on the far side of the river were probably working at this time and would have been clearly visible from the river walk in Temple Grounds.) The example is unusual, but not unique; a series of ponds belonging to an ironworks became ornamental ponds in the park of Attingham Hall, Shropshire (Bettey 1993, 90 – 2), for instance.

STANWICK

A potentially more instructive example is provided by the earthworks at Stanwick, about 8 miles (13 km) to the north of Richmond. The extensive late Iron Age site of Stanwick, with its massive ramparts and ditches, is surely one of the most impressive prehistoric sites in the north of England. Since the 1950s archaeological perceptions of Stanwick have been coloured by Sir Mortimer Wheeler's account of his excavations there (1954). Wheeler, and other commentators, have treated Stanwick as a single period, Iron Age, phenomenon; there is no mention of the later landscapes in Wheeler's report. Yet it is clear that these ramparts formed a significant element in the landscape in all subsequent periods, affecting the layout of medieval settlements, but more particularly, for the purposes of this paper, in the landscapes of the two neighbouring 18th-century parks of Forcett Hall and Stanwick Hall. Detailed archaeological field survey by the RCHME has elucidated some details of the design of these parks.

Forcett Hall was designed by Daniel Garrett for Richard Shuttleworth in about 1740; the identity of the park designer is not known but it

23

may have been Thomas Wright of Durham (Harris 1971). Stanwick Hall, demolished earlier this century, was a 17th-century house remodelled extensively in the 1740s. William Kent, Daniel Garrett and Thomas Wright were probably involved in this work which was undertaken by Elizabeth, later 1st Duchess of Northumberland, immediately upon her marriage to Sir Hugh Smithson, the owner of Stanwick. The Duchess was an architecture-and-design enthusiast and Garrett was her protégé (Percy and Jackson-Stops 1974, 193). Further additions were made by Decimus Burton in 1842.

In both parks the designers made good use of the prehistoric earthworks where they formed the boundaries of the new landscapes. The following paragraphs are based upon the detailed description by Welfare *et al* (1990, 20–33).

The western ramparts of the Iron Age site formed the eastern side of Forcett Park (Fig 14). From Forcett Church southwards to the lake the Iron Age ditch became a ha-ha and the rampart crest was reduced, widened and given a smooth gradient to become a carriage drive known as Church Walk. Beyond this, at the end of the lake, the line of the bank is incorporated in the mid 18th-century dam, though it is not known how much of the Iron Age fabric survives within this

structure. To the south of the lake the bank has been further graded as a raised carriage drive, of impressive proportions, providing good views in all directions except to the south; it is, in effect, a linear prospect mound. The extent of the 18th-century remodelling can be seen just below the crest of the hill where the ditch bows outwards but the carriage drive continues straight. At the top of the hill the carriage drive turns west and can be seen running along the crest giving views over the whole park. The prehistoric ramparts also turn west at this point, possibly forming an everted entrance, while to the south, where the ramparts are much reduced, there was no carriage drive but there does seem to have been a raised footpath. The OS first edition map of 1854 shows a grotto on the line of the bank, now marked only by a hollow, which is skirted by the path, levelling the ditch. A further 90 m to the south, the crest of the bank has been modified to create a platform revetted by a semi-circular wall; the date and function of this is unknown but it could have accommodated a garden ornament or seat.

Turning to Stanwick Park; a summer house in the south-western corner of the park is probably part of the 1740s landscaping, but is now overgrown with ivy. It was located at the junction

Figure 14
Stanwick, N. Yorkshire: a simplified plan showing features mentioned in the text (RCHME, © Crown copyright)

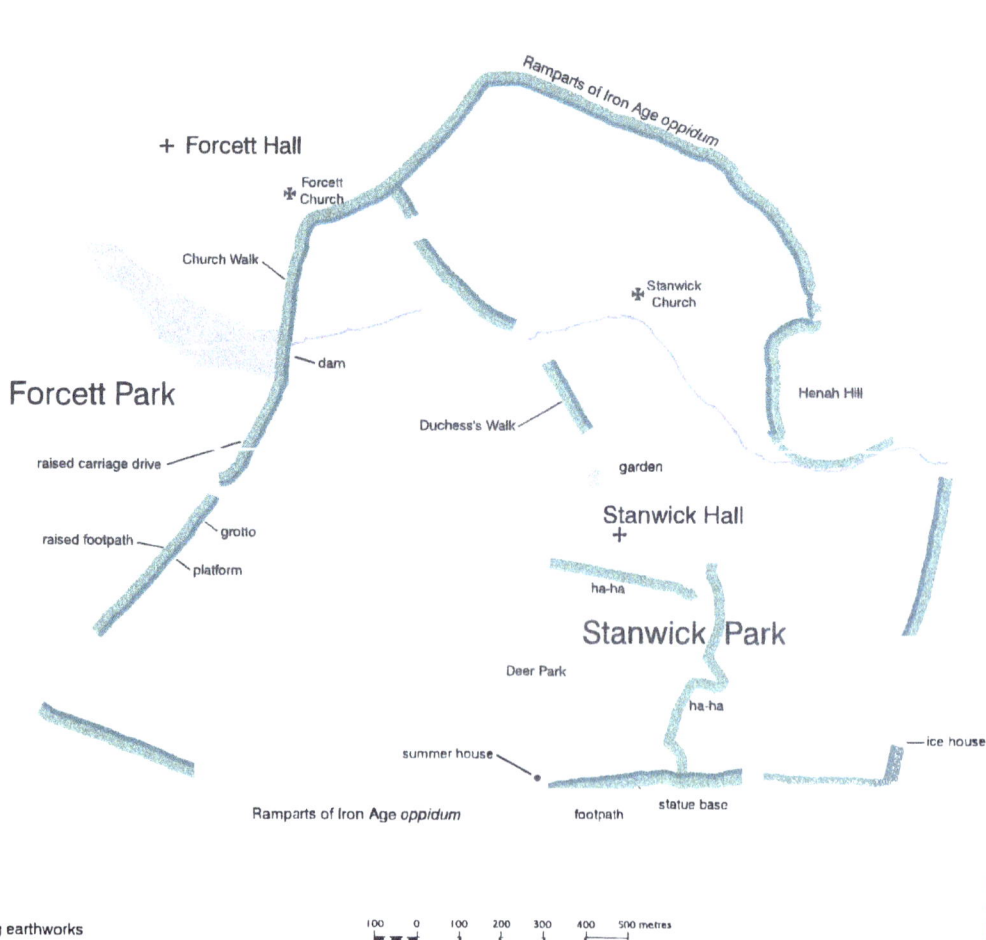

of two carriage drives and at a point which gives excellent views across the park, especially in afternoon light. The top of the adjacent Iron Age rampart appears to have been graded for use as a path over a distance of about 300 m. At the eastern end of this path a dressed stone base, probably for a statue, has been placed on the crest of the bank. From the south-eastern corner of the Deer Park onwards the ramparts have largely been levelled. This was done before 1816 (Whitaker 1823, opp 207) but it is not known whether this was part of the 1740s landscaping scheme; no obvious purpose connected with that scheme seems to have been served. Just north of the south-eastern corner the rampart has been pushed into the ditch and a slight hollow marks subsidence into an ice-house, marked on Richard Richardson's estate map of 1772 (Duke of Northumberland's archives, Alnwick Castle X.III.10.41).

The relative sharpness of the earthworks of the Duchess's Walk, otherwise known as The Terrace, suggests some more recent remodelling. This section of the earthworks also differs from the other Iron Age ramparts in being very straight. This area lay outside Stanwick Park in the 1740s so the ornamental walk here is presumably of a later date, probably in the early or mid 19th century. The Duchess referred to was probably Eleanor, wife of the 4th Duke. Within the garden a break in the line of the bank, just a south-facing scarp here, marks the position of a conservatory marked on the 1772 and 1854 maps. Further east the line of the bank is marked by a polygonal mound, presumably a garden feature, possibly carved out of the bank. The modifications to the Iron Age earthworks here, amounting to severe mutilation, are undated and may be associated with the 17th-century house rather than, or as well as, the later works.

DISCUSSION

Two major questions arise from all this. The first one is, what do these modifications tell us about the prehistoric earthworks? Secondly, and more importantly for these proceedings, what meaning did the prehistoric features have in the 18th century? The first question has two strands, which can only be dealt with briefly here. An understanding of the park designs can help us to appreciate why the prehistoric earthworks appear as they do: why certain sections have been reduced and others altered. More significantly, the reuse of elements of the ramparts for a very different purpose in the 18th century may give us some clues as to their original purpose. Several archaeologists have found Stanwick unconvincing as a defensive site; in particular, the way in which the excellent prospects afforded by the western ramparts have been used by the park designers, helps to highlight the fact that the

ramparts at Stanwick give good views in all directions, and that they look inwards as much as outwards. Stanwick is the enclosure of a low-lying valley, as are many other Iron Age *oppida* and related sites; this inward-looking aspect may help us to explain the otherwise inexplicable exclusion of Henah Hill from the circuit. It may indicate that the ramparts were built with an emphasis on social prestige and possibly for other, enigmatic reasons, rather than simply for defence. (The same considerations may apply in an opposite sense in the case of Culloden Tower at Richmond – its prominent situation would have provided a good strategic location in the medieval period, lending support to Clarkson's statement (1821, 328)).

To return to the second question: were the ramparts of Stanwick numinous to the park designers and their patrons, or were they merely convenient? I ask this question in a spirit of pure enquiry and in the hope of promoting the kind of dialogue which Christopher Taylor (this volume) is asking for.

Elsewhere, as is very well known, the gothick was much sought after in park design, as seen, for instance, in Humphry Repton's scheme of 1792 for Mulgrave Castle on the North York Moors (NMR No NZ 81 SW 4); and there was nothing so gothick as an abbey, as Catherine Morland was well aware (Jane Austen, *Northanger Abbey*, chapter 17 *et passim*). At another outstanding North Yorkshire site the ruins of Fountains Abbey (NMR No SE 26 NE 3) form the backdrop to the Aislabies' park at Studley Royal, created in the 1720s, and there are, perhaps, even better examples of the selective retention of monastic building fabric, as, for example, at Tupholme, Lincolnshire (Everson 1996b, 15).

But could the Iron Age earthworks at Stanwick have held any similar meaning? Unfortunately, little is known about the tastes and interests of the Shuttleworths of Forcett Hall. Elizabeth, Duchess of Northumberland, on the other hand, is a well-documented figure (Percy and Jackson-Stops 1974). An indefatigable commentator on other people's houses and parks, she approved of what has been called 'highly artificial rusticity' in the rococo style, with plenty of follies, grottoes and similar ornaments; but she also developed a taste for the gothick and the romantic, admiring the dramatic Northumberland coastal landscape at Dunstanburgh Castle, for instance, in 1760 (*ibid* 310). This has a clear connection with her patronage of Garrett, master of the blending of rococo and gothick. Unfortunately, the works at Stanwick which might be attributable to the 1st Duchess tended largely towards the destruction, rather than the enhancement, of the prehistoric earthworks. Generally, it is in the less well–documented Forcett Park that the earthworks were more positively treated; the only hint we have is that it was possibly the same design team of Garrett and Wright which may have been employed in both parks, and that Thomas Wright, at least, had an interest in antiquities. He wrote about what he believed to be Druidical, Roman and Saxon remains in England and was knowledgeable concerning classical antiquity. He was also acquainted with such antiquaries as Roger Gale. Much later, in the 19th century, when the Duchess's Walk was laid out at Stanwick, we know that there was an active interest in the archaeology of the locality, partly stimulated by the discovery of the Stanwick hoard at Melsonby (Haselgrove *et al* 1990, 11–13). The 4th Duke was a leading antiquarian and employed Henry MacLauchlan – a pioneer of archaeological field survey (Charlton and Day 1984) – who produced a plan of the Stanwick earthworks in 1849. But even before this the earthworks had been surveyed in 1816 by Thomas Bradley for Whitaker's *History of Richmondshire* (1823).

There are hints elsewhere in the country that earthworks of antiquity were deliberately and consciously incorporated into parks. This is certainly the case with burial mounds. At Greenwich a cemetery of Anglo-Saxon barrows was apparently respected and retained as a feature within the Royal Park while a mound marking the site of a Roman temple, which may have been viewed in a similar light, was treated as a focus for a formal avenue (Pattison this volume). A further example is a bell barrow (NMR No SU 13 NW 38) overlooking Lake House, Wiltshire, which has been remodelled to form a spectacular prospect mound.

Other designed gardens which incorporated ancient earthworks include Mavisbank, Midlothian, the estate of Sir John Clerk, another acquaintance of Gale and Stukeley, where the gardens incorporate an 'ancient trench & agger' (Spink 1974, 31, 34–5). This is a fort which was believed by Clerk to be of Roman date but which is almost certainly prehistoric (RCAHMS 1929, 116, no. 144). At Downton, Wiltshire, a medieval castle ringwork-and-bailey became the basis for a complex series of formal gardens (Humphrey Welfare pers comm).

Another Iron Age site which became the location for post-medieval gardens is Vespasian's Camp, Wiltshire, incorporated in the park of Amesbury House and landscaped in the mid 18th century (RCHME 1979, xx-xxi, 20–2). The hillfort formed the focus for Bridgeman's plan for the enlarged park in 1738 (Bold 1988, 106). The interior was modified by this landscaping and by previous cultivation, but the ramparts were also modified by the construction of paths and a grotto, Gay's Cave. A further example, recently studied by the RCHME, may be St Ann's Hill, Surrey (McOmish and Field 1994), though that was not landscaped as a garden until the early Victorian period, when the eastern rampart of the hillfort was partly levelled and incorporated into a path leading to the summer house which occupied the site of St Ann's Chapel (David McOmish pers comm).

The meaning invested in ruins and prehistoric remains in the 18th century no doubt depended on the views of the individuals in question; one only has to think, for instance, of the strong differences of opinion between Repton and the protagonists of the picturesque, satirised in Thomas Love Peacock's *Headlong Hall*. We need to know more about the owners and designers who used ancient earthworks in their parks and gardens: their education, their acquaintance, their reading, their experience, their collections, what they were thinking and what they were trying to achieve with their landscapes.

Perhaps the only answer which I can offer at present to my own question, 'were the ramparts at Stanwick numinous?', is a very broad one. If the designers of the parks at Forcett and Stanwick took note of Alexander Pope's injunction to 'consult the genius of the place in all' (*Epistle IV: to Richard Boyle, Earl of Burlington: of the Use of Riches,* line 57), as they surely did (being members of the Burlington set), they can hardly have failed to recognise the genius of the place in the massive, and still enigmatic, earthworks of the late Iron Age *oppidum*. The genius could reside in artificial, as well as in natural features. (And would a concern for the genius of the place, to those with a classical education, have implied something more, in terms of divinity, spirituality or awe, than a recognition of the 'capabilities' of a landscape which Brown saw?). Of course, to consult the genius of the place is not to leave it respectfully untouched; designers must design. The alterations which we see in the ramparts at Stanwick are not incompatible with a recognition of the genius of the place – indeed, as suggested above, I think they have highlighted it.

ACKNOWLEDGEMENTS

This paper is based on an idea by Humphrey Welfare. I would also like to acknowledge a debt to my colleagues Paul Everson and David McOmish for fruitful discussion of the subject. Thanks are also due to participants at the conference who made useful comments, particularly Mr John Phibbs, Mr Tom La Dell, Dr Norman Hammond and Mrs Valerie Hepworth. Figure 14 was prepared by Moraig Brown.

RECORDING WHAT ISN'T THERE: THREE DIFFICULTIES WITH 18TH-CENTURY LANDSCAPES

John Phibbs

ABSTRACT

The field archaeology of parks and gardens looks straightforward. It fits existing systems of recording. Gardens are usually rectilinear; parterres are symmetrical; mounts circular. They make sense to the eye when they are drawn up. Parks are even easier; a few bits of field boundary, some ridge and furrow, and an overlay of ha-has, avenues and drives. At Wimpole, Cambridgeshire, the field archaeology is easy and informative because the designed landscape retained its agricultural framework. If we are very clever we can plot the ornamental planting as well and analyse its habit to extend the record into areas where the land-form is too faint to capture directly.

In fact, we have grounds for complacency in our recording techniques. I know of only one hole in the smiling fabric, it is large and roughly Capability Brown shaped. Perhaps 'very large' would better define the problem, because Brownian landscape means very large-scale and extensive earth moving. Archaeologists have in general not tackled this problem.

RECORDING THE MISSING EARTHWORKS

In a perfect world there would be close kinship between medieval countryside and 18th-century landscape: the hill, once a landmark for the setting out of ancient roads and fields, becoming the focal point of a network of avenues; the stream metamorphosed to a lake; the arable valleys, through which it flows, carrying the lawns of a great house. The romantic movement that so influenced landscape design in the 18th century would have endorsed the Platonic idea that beneath the crust of appearance there is some inherent shadow of ideal country, a *genius loci* perhaps, to which all people of all times must respond, no matter what their purpose.

Such seamless development from agriculture into landscape is readily interpreted with the traditional skills of field archaeology; the trouble is that the world is rarely perfect, indeed I have only ever found perfection of this kind at Wimpole, Cambridgeshire (Fig 15).

Whereas at Wimpole many of the medieval earthworks survived more or less intact until the 1980s, one of the effects of most landscaping is to remove or modify them. There are ways in which an archaeologist can circumvent this problem: trees and shrubs can help – to stay with Wimpole for a moment longer – one or two thorn stumps survive along a deer park boundary which was abandoned over 200 years ago and prove the existence of something otherwise only recorded on sketch plans.

In most landscapes of any size there will be areas of parkland where field boundaries survive not as banks but as irregular rows of field boundary oak and elm. At Wanstead, Essex, the RCHME plotted holly and thorn trees, many of them quite insignificant, and found an astonishing coincidence with the lines of walks and vistas made *c* 1700 (NMR No TQ 48 NW 82).

By ring counting stumps and by carefully recording the sizes and habits of trees and shrubs we can also come to some conclusion about their date, origin and function (the height of the hedge or shrubbery and whether or not the tree has been transplanted from a neighbouring hedge or plantation). Notwithstanding the terrors of plant identification, these skills are a natural extension of the field archaeologist's work: they enable features that have otherwise disappeared to be recorded, and it is devoutly to be wished that in consequence, some trees may be accorded a measure of protection (for example, old pollards).

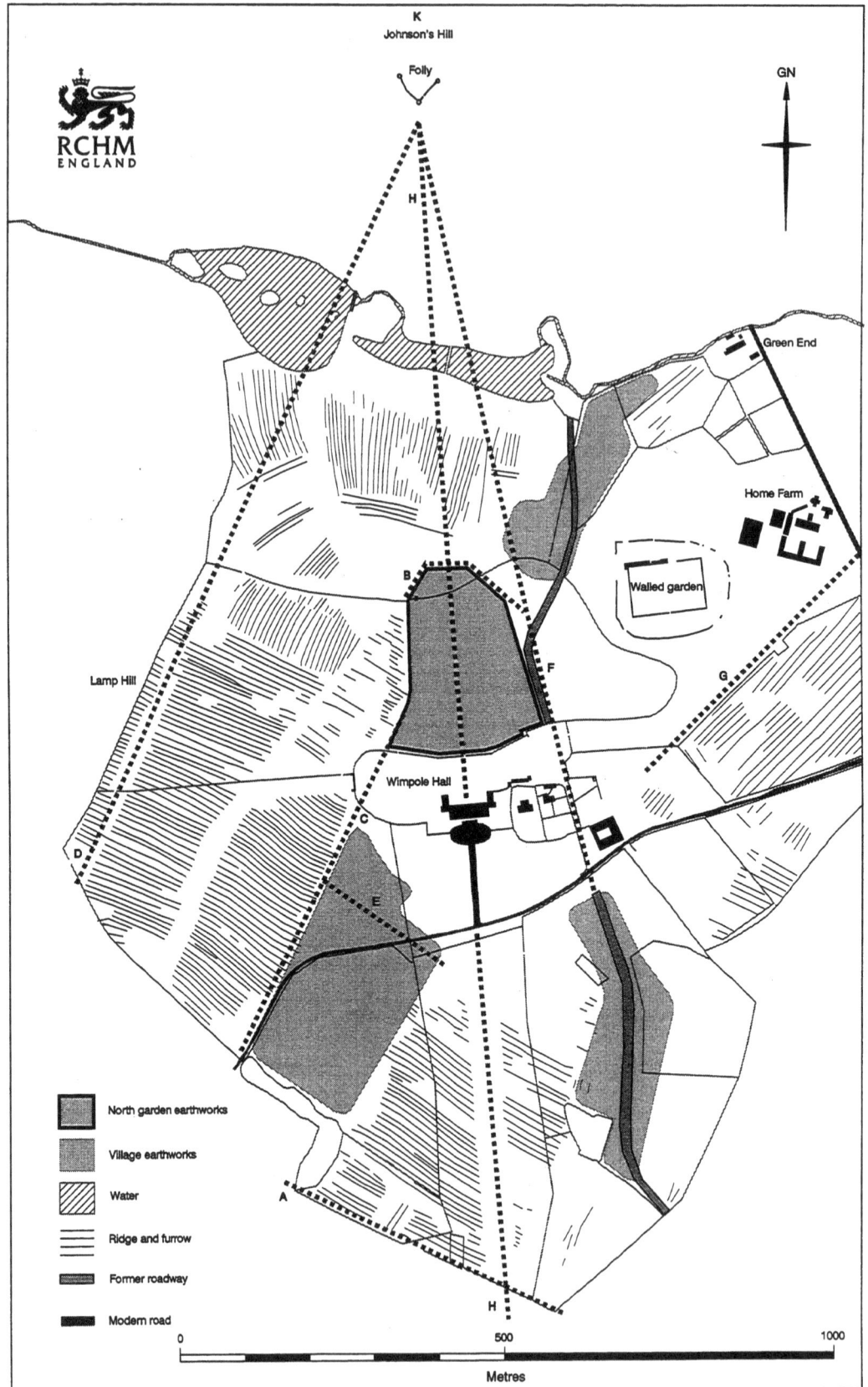

Figure 15
Wimpole, Cambridgeshire. To an unusual degree the intricate formal landscape of Wimpole grew out of its agricultural antecedents. This evolution takes three forms.
1 The understandable reuse of field boundaries as park boundaries and of medieval trees as the basis of ornamental clumps.
2 The use of drives and field boundaries to provide the alignments and orientation of the formal design (the ha-ha, A on the plan, took the line of the earlier Rushbrooke Way; the formal garden north of the house was determined by Wimpole Way, B; the Walnut Avenue, C, was laid out along another old road; further old roads, E, determined the water gardens; while still another determined the south boundary of the later pleasure ground, G).
3 Even at its grandest, the formal design follows the medieval landscape, for both seem to focus on Johnson's Hill (K). Thus the north–south axis of the house (H), whose construction pre-dates the incorporation of the hill into the park, nonetheless runs to it; as does the old headland along Lamp Hill (D), which had an avenue planted down it, and the old Wimpole Way (F) which was adopted as the east wall of the formal garden (RCHME, © Crown copyright).

RECORDING WHAT IS MISSING FROM THE EARTHWORKS

The 18th century, however, raises bigger issues than this, and most relevant to archaeologists is the place of apparently relict medieval elements within designed landscape. Parkland is often regarded as a reservoir teeming with the archaeology of medieval and ancient life, but why should this be so?

Let us consider the extremes of ridged cultivation and ruins. I have tried again and again to reconcile ridge and furrow with designed landscape, two of the more promising lines of thought run as follows:

1 Ridge and furrow in 18th-century grassland management:

Ridge and furrow was still very much a part of agriculture in the 18th century. This is well known to archaeologists of course, but in many texts it is still described as 'relict medieval open field', and it may be worth emphasising how misleading this can be. Ridge and furrow in 18th-century parkland was neither 'relict' – it may have been in use – nor 'medieval' because it is clear from 18th-century accounts that ridge and furrow was regularly 'cast' (ie ploughed out) and remade. This practice was not regarded as a great cost, so there is no telling when a piece had last been arched up. Nor was ridge and furrow necessarily 'part of the open field system' – it is not always easy to distinguish ridge and furrow made for arable cropping from that made for pasture. In 18th-century landscape then, ridge and furrow does not necessarily survive from an obsolete system that no one had bothered to clear up, but was useful cheap land drainage. One would only expect it to be done away with where its presence detracted from views and the setting of buildings. Indeed, I have slight evidence that some was made within established parkland.

Ridge and furrow was valued by 18th-century agriculturists for laying wet land dry (Young 1786, 111; Young 1791b, 495; Young 1793, 68); as a way of increasing the surface area of a grass field (Young 1790, 249–250) and as a cheap way of preparing arable ground (Young 1786, 112; Young 1791, 495). It was also regarded as a way of draining grassland specifically (Walker 1795, 21; Villiers 1804) and was widespread in the treatment of grassland, in the Midlands and in Northamptonshire in particular (Young 1791, 495; Repton 1791). Among the writers that I have read, only Marshall and Kent refer to the practice as medieval and as a possible agricultural problem (Marshall 1804, 258–9). For Kent, and for a description of the Flanders style of construction, see Young (1797, 33).

2 Grassland as an indicator of antiquity:

William Beckford wrote to Franchi on 16 June 1811, concerning Bitham Lake, newly made within the barrier at Fonthill, Wiltshire:

> *Here everything is gradually lapsing into antiquity – grass up to the very doors etc. The lake looks as if God had made it, it is so natural ... the swans look as if they are in Paradise (Alexander 1957).*

If grassland was brought up to the house for the associations this had with a Claudian reading of antiquity, then one might judge that ridge and furrow was retained for the same reason (namely as the shadow of a by-gone agricultural industry).

While the meaning of ridge and furrow in designed landscape remains obscure, it does seem to me that we should record *inter alia* its condition. This point can be made more clearly in the context of ruins: archaeologists and historians are always under pressure to regard ruins (be they military, like Sherborne Castle, Dorset, or ecclesiastical, like Roche Abbey, Yorkshire) as a survival most significant to the period that built them. Whatever light they may shed on medieval life, we know that most ruins were messed around with in the 18th century, either by further destruction or by additions (as Repton added to Mulgrave Castle, Yorkshire, and Gilpin to Crom Castle, Fermanagh), in order to form picturesque masses of masonry.

Whatever our interpretation of the place of medieval monuments and earthworks in designed landscapes, we should therefore aim to record not only what survives from the time when they were built, but also the way they have been treated since, and how and why they were slighted. The physical context in which they are analysed must be extended beyond the medieval precinct and the open field system, into the whole landscape of which they were later made a part (Fig 16).

This goes beyond the use of trees as a record of missing earthworks and demands more from the archaeologist. It encourages two unsettling conclusions: first, that ridge and furrow and ruins must, on occasion, be more valued the more ruinous they are; and second, that ridge and furrow is often an integral part of 18th-century parkland, with implications for the landscaping at every level from the composition of views to the texture of the flora. Therefore, where we plan to replant and restore that parkland, we should consider reinstating the ridge and furrow that has been ploughed away in this century.

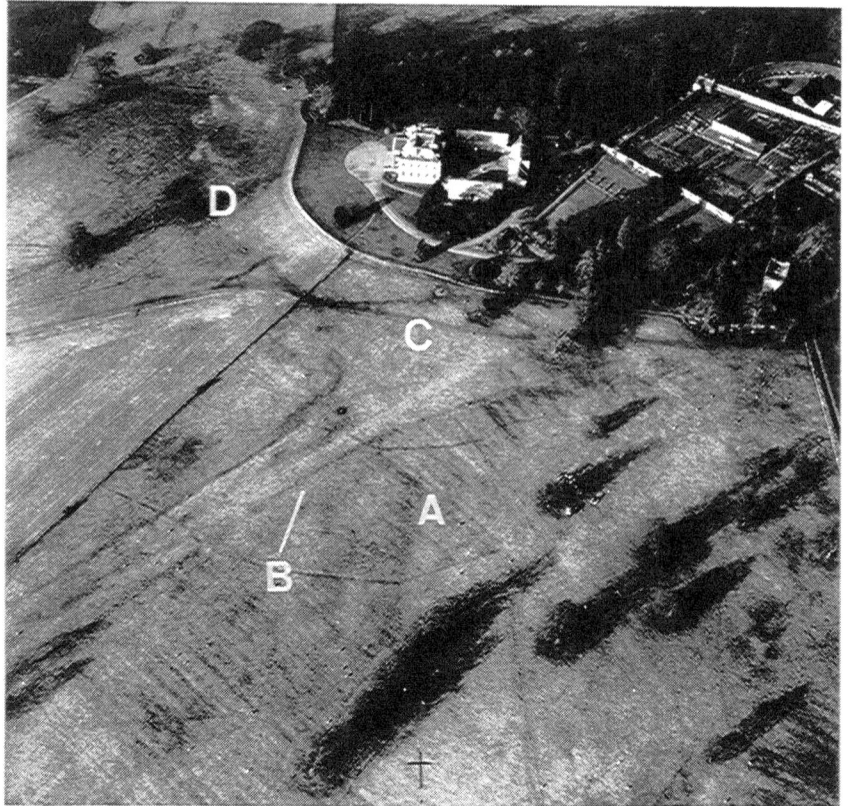

Figure 16
Aerial photograph of Berrington Hall, Herefordshire. In the lower half of the picture the ridge and furrow is extensive, A. It is stopped by the trace of a sunk fence (infilled about 1841) that runs from the walled garden to 8 o'clock, B. However, traces of the ridge and furrow can still be seen near the house above the sunk fence, C. These traces may be more revealing of Brownian landscape than the rest. The pale marks to the left of the house look like Brownian infilling, D. The park has been ploughed since the photograph was taken and little of the ridge and furrow survives, however it was very conspicuous in the landscape, and we should consider reinstating it (Cambridge University Committee for Aerial Photography BLG 41, 15 December 1972).

RECORDING THE MISSING EARTH

This second leap of the imagination into the recording of what is not there, is itself belittled by a third which cuts deep into the foggy heart of parkland archaeology. I must ask archaeologists to look at that great comfort blanket that is summoned up by the phrase 'swept away': as in 'the formal garden, village, roads, entire medieval record etc. etc. were swept away by Capability Brown'.

There are three reasons for reconsidering our use of the phrase: first, because 18th-century landscaping was seldom so radical; second, because it begs the question 'swept away by what?'; and third because it appears to make intellectually plausible the usual archaeological response to landscaping on a Brownian scale: that is, say nothing, do nothing, leave plan blank. In Brownian landscape *en fin*, the sensible archaeologist stops where the serious archaeology starts.

Tom Williamson has shown at length how complex 18th-century development was and how much of what was already there was retained (Williamson 1995, 68–100), but even where Brownian landscape is at its most sweeping, its earthworks remain formidable – vast prostrate sculptures. Therefore, to dismiss them unrecorded as 'sweeping away' is akin to turning from a Henry Moore and saying 'pity about the marble'. If we look for scale, ambition and attention to detail in landscaping, then the work of the late

18th century is far more to be valued, nationally and internationally, than anything that came before it. The emphasis that current archaeology puts on formal layouts of the 16th to 18th centuries has temporarily blinded us to this obvious fact.

How then are we to go about recording these landscapes? Even archaeologists find Brownian earthworks very hard to see, let alone interpret, and this may account for their rarity in the record: Christopher Taylor has plotted the earthworks at Madingley, Cambridgeshire and Dominic Cole (a landscape architect) has shown how the Grecian valley was excavated at Stowe, Buckinghamshire, and the soil used to fill the lawn between the house and lake. Elsewhere, large-scale Brownian earthworks may occasionally have been mapped as part of another exercise.

The work has to be conducted both at large and small scales. At the large scale, as at Stowe, it would be useful to establish where the earth was before the Brownian work began. We can then draw up a 'heat map', to show where he spent his money and which parts were left alone. Much of the most revealing earthworking, however, was carried out at a very small scale. For example, linear banks no more than 150 mm high to conceal the approach at Heveningham, Suffolk, and carefully contoured mounds or tumps for planting at Croome, Wiltshire. To recognise and map these we need first to establish a vocabulary for the earthworks which will explain their function in the landscape. Within my own practice,

Debois, we have for some years been trying to develop this, with 'middle ground terraces', 'upcast' and 'downcast' roads etc (Phibbs 1994).

To recognise that these earthworks exist and have meaning is one thing, to draw them is another. For instance, at Himley, Staffordshire, and Weald, Essex, there are steady levelled gradients a quarter mile or more in length running from the house to the water – features far too large and gradual for conventional depiction – and similarly, at Highclere, Hampshire, there is an excavated lawn with smaller valleys inscribed into its sides. Contouring helps, but is never adequate for the subtlety of the shapes. In our own work we have tried to forget archaeology and sketch the landform without regard to its human or natural origin. It is usually more immediately important to know whether a gradient could have taken a drive, or whether a hill-top could be flat enough to have been used as a viewpoint, than to decide whether or not these things were man-made. I suspect that for a full interpretation the standard practice of mapping earthworks in plan may itself have to be amended: many Brownian earthworks are incoherent in plan and can only be read in relation to particular planting effects and particular viewpoints.

Because they leave so little behind them and are not easy to predict, in the way that the fourth wall of a rectangular building is, small-scale Brownian earthworks are particularly vulnerable to the extensive ploughing of post-war agriculture. As techniques for rectifying oblique aerial photographs improve however, it may be possible to use photographs taken in the 1940s and 1950s to calculate the pre-war ground levels, and then compare these with modern ground levels before considering the reinstatement of the earthworks.

It may also be possible to record parkland landscapes using XYZ data, formed into 3-D digital ground models on computer, to provide oblique aerial and perspective views. Specific landscape or archaeological features might be highlighted on these models, and GIS offer opportunities to layer such interpretative material over the basic model (Paul Pattison pers comm).

SOME FINAL POINTS

Earthworks for which we have no record, no language and no understanding can find no place in conservation policy. Such is their vulnerability that I have even come across ha-has, the single most important technical device of the Brownian park, filled in or redug on new lines with the complicity of government agencies. Archaeologists should enable themselves to take a view on this matter.

In this short piece I have several times referred to the possibility of reinstating earthworks. I am aware of the precedent such a practice may set, and of the risks to archaeology, but the issue deserves discussion and archaeology should address itself to the future of the monuments that it records.

This is an exciting time in garden history, there is an 18th-century banquet on the table, we should not spend the whole night fiddling with the 17th-century lettuce.

'DELIGHTFULLY SURROUNDED WITH WOODS AND PONDS': FIELD EVIDENCE FOR MEDIEVAL GARDENS IN ENGLAND
Paul Everson

ABSTRACT

Plausible examples of the field remains of medieval gardens in England are still rare but growing in numbers. Recognition of such field evidence for medieval gardens has progressed by steps of increasingly confident perception, typically reassessing already well-documented field monuments, rather than by outright new discoveries.

Such gardens have several characteristics in common. The importance of approach; the manipulation of water – to surround, to reflect, to support imagery, to sustain fish and birds that carry their own symbolism; the close integration of their built element and the capacity to surprise and delight or to create an image. Non-fieldwork studies, have helped to define the typical elements and thereby aid their recognition.

This paper outlines several examples where field survey has thrown up new insights to aspects of design in medieval landscape. It also makes tentative suggestions for further exploration and research. In conclusion, it proposes that the results of field survey around great medieval buildings can only be fully appreciated via an understanding of the imagery and symbolism which was an integral part of their creation. Garden historians have a key role to play in this process.

This paper perforce owes its detailed content to many colleagues and friends. In bringing together their fieldwork, observations and comments, it aims by juxtaposition to take a developing subject a little further and to make its potential interest more widely known.

'The quest for the medieval garden is tantalising'. The opening sentence of Sylvia Landsberg's elegant recent book on the subject (Landsberg 1995) is a sentiment that strikes a chord with field archaeologists. The merest handful of examples of the small-scale enclosed gardens, closely integrated with residential ranges – the type that figures principally in our traditional conception of medieval gardens – have been identified as abandoned field remains. One such is at the site of the Bishop of Lincoln's medieval palace at Nettleham, near Lincoln (Everson, Taylor and Dunn 1991, 129–31). Yet recent work by field archaeologists in England has begun to suggest that what is required to break this impasse is rather a refocusing of expectation and perception than outright new discoveries. And it is the generous acknowledgement and encouragement of these developments by Sylvia Landsberg and other garden historians that lends them some impetus and, one might say, credibility.

The quotation within this paper's title comes from the 12th-century account by Giraldus Cambrensis of St Hugh of Lincoln's first visit to another episcopal palace and hunting park, at Stow Park, 10 miles (16 km) north west of Lincoln. It conveniently encapsulates several aspects of medieval gardens as designed landscapes – more akin, therefore, to 18th-century creations than to the *hortus conclusus* – that could reasonably be identified in the degraded field remains at Stow Park (Everson, Taylor and Dunn 1991, 184–5). They include an approach along the highway of the former Roman road, giving views across a shallow valley to the palace and its large hunting park stretching away behind to the south. Closer, there was an axial approach between extensive sheets of water; with perhaps an enclosed or pleasure garden to one side containing small ponds. There was perhaps too, a wooded backdrop, but certainly there were woodland blocks within the park and in extensive belts along its bounds. Yet the hagiographic thrust of Giraldus's story, about how Hugh's approach was greeted by the flight of the resident flock of swans in the face of a marvellous newcomer, confirms the presence of additional levels of symbolism in the site's less fixed appurtenances. Swans could indeed sustain a complex network of symbolism:

sincerity from their whiteness, hence also purity and grace that might evoke the Virgin; they could be a Christian emblem of retirement, but also a part of the teeming variety and wonder of all creation; they were routinely part of the intertwined imagery of hunting rituals and courtly love as well as evoking the early legend of the Swan Knight with its dynastic significance (Klingender 1971, *passim*; Cherry 1969). This can only have acquired additional significance by the adoption of the swan as the emblem of Lincoln's greatest bishop and saint.

Plausible examples of field remains of such medieval designed landscapes in England are still rare, but growing in numbers. Recognition of such field evidence has progressed by steps of increasingly confident perception, typically reassessing already well-documented field monuments through detailed field survey, rather than outright discoveries of sites new to the archaeological record. Intelligent perception, more than additional scarps or more documentation, was the key to the refocused understanding, through RCHME fieldwork, at sites such as Stow Park, Somersham Palace (Taylor 1989) and Bodiam Castle (Taylor, Everson and Wilson-North 1990). In the latter instance, the earthworks surrounding Sir Edward Dallingridge's newly created residence, with its licence to crenellate of 1385, indeed show in a remarkable way how the perceptions of contemporary visitors were manipulated, stimulated and presumably delighted by the elaborately contrived access. But also those perceptions were specifically focused – as Charles Coulson (1992) has convincingly articulated – on emblems of castellation and chivalry contained in architectural forms, details and decoration that were precisely suited to evoke Dallingridge's career of military service to the English crown in France and his *arriviste* assertion of social position.

Sites where this categorisation and form of analysis apparently has a place, and where there are earthwork remains of a deliberately designed setting, form a growing catalogue in the minds of interested scholars (see Taylor this volume). Following the signpost offered by Stow Park and Somersham, rural archiepiscopal and episcopal residences are likely to have shared similar characteristics to greater or lesser extent, as fieldwork at Cawood (Blood and Taylor 1992), Alvechurch (Aston 1970–72) and Bishop's Waltham (Hare 1988), for example, has indeed shown. Functionally comparable, but less pretentious residences of other ecclesiastics have aspects of their location and setting that ought properly to be viewed in this way, like the great pond at the prior of Wenlock's house and park at Great Oxenbold in Shropshire (see below and Fig 21).

Many are castles, in name, form and pretension; and progress in this field goes hand-in-hand with the growing realisation that castle buildings are not just (or even sometimes not at all) military structures and that their primary meanings may be to do with landscape and other symbolism (Stocker 1993). They range from those large in scale and well known from documentation or surviving structures like Kenilworth with its massive former mere, or Leeds or Framlingham also with large meres, through examples like Cooling, Bolingbroke, Stokesay and Clun castles, to smaller, more obscure and wholly earthwork sites such as Pan Castle, near Whitchurch in Shropshire (NMR SJ 54 SW 12), where a natural mere (now drained) seems to have formed part of the setting. At a few, close study of standing structures has been integrated with a consideration of the manipulated setting and the interplay of the two aspects. Clun exemplifies this, where the earthworks of its water garden and lake in the valley below have been crucial to the arguments about the non-military character of the keep-like lodging range (work by the City of Hereford Archaeology Unit, see Morriss 1990; Nenk, Margeson and Hurley 1993, 279–80; and see also Stamper 1996, plate 4). The whole grouping plausibly seeks a particular effect when viewed from the road out of Wales (Barratt 1994). Increasing numbers of similar sites are likely to be recognised through systematic re-examination of earthworks hitherto only simply categorised. Whorlton Castle in North Yorkshire and Shotwick Castle in Cheshire display such characteristics and further examples are emerging in some parts of the country as a result of the site re-evaluations inherent in the progress of English Heritage's Monuments Protection Programme (Went 1986a; 1986b, for example).

There is a study waiting to be undertaken on these water castles alone, both individually and as a thematic group. They have obvious characteristics in common. The importance of approach; the manipulation of water – to surround, to reflect, to support imagery, to sustain fish and birds that carry their own symbolism; the close integration of their built element, with its own range of imagery; the capacity to surprise and delight or to create an impression. An additional feature of prime relevance is the creation of external viewpoints from which the designed landscape could be advantageously viewed. This is stunningly present at Bodiam, in the nearby earthwork platform known as the Gun Garden (Taylor, Everson and Wilson-North 1990; see Everson 1996a, fig 4) and apparently at Somersham (Taylor 1989, 217). Such occurrences, if at all as common as the topographical context of many sites suggests, reflect a medieval sensibility about landscape setting that might hitherto have seemed surprising (Leslie 1993).

Recent RCHME site survey tasks continue to throw up new insights in this field and illustrate its potential. At Whorlton Castle in North Yorkshire (Figs 17 and 18) what appears to have been

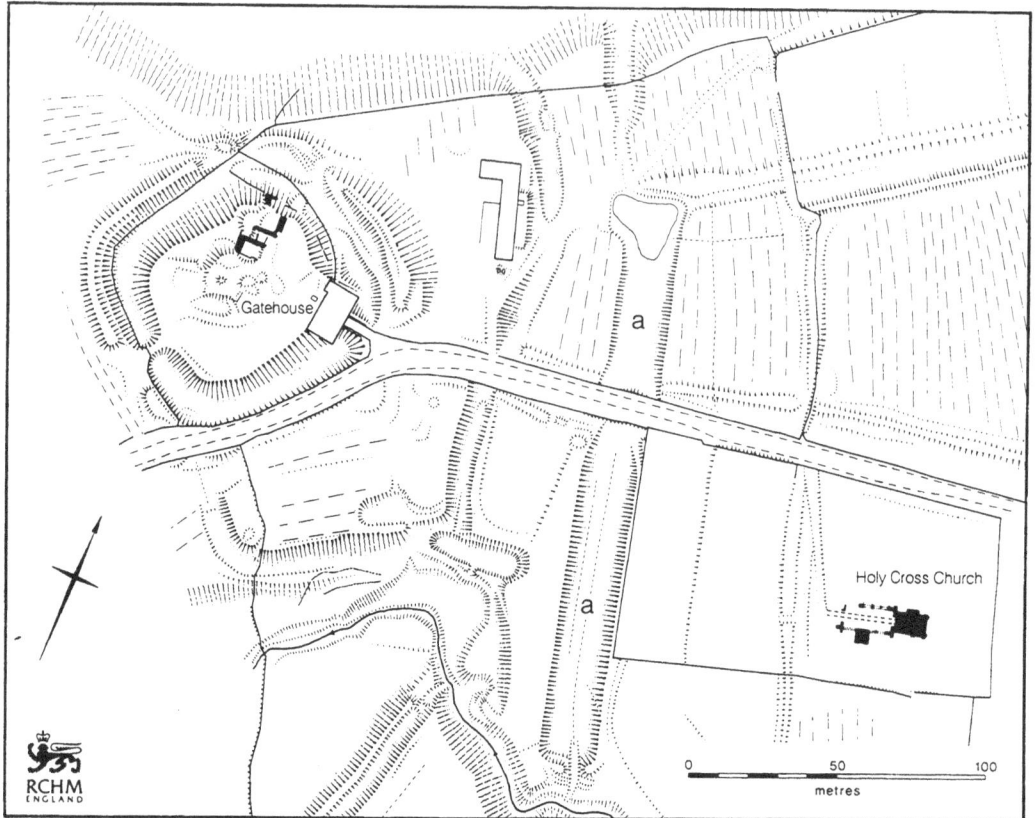

Figure 17
Whorlton Castle, North Yorkshire: extract from the survey plan, original at 1:1 000 scale (RCHME, © Crown copyright).

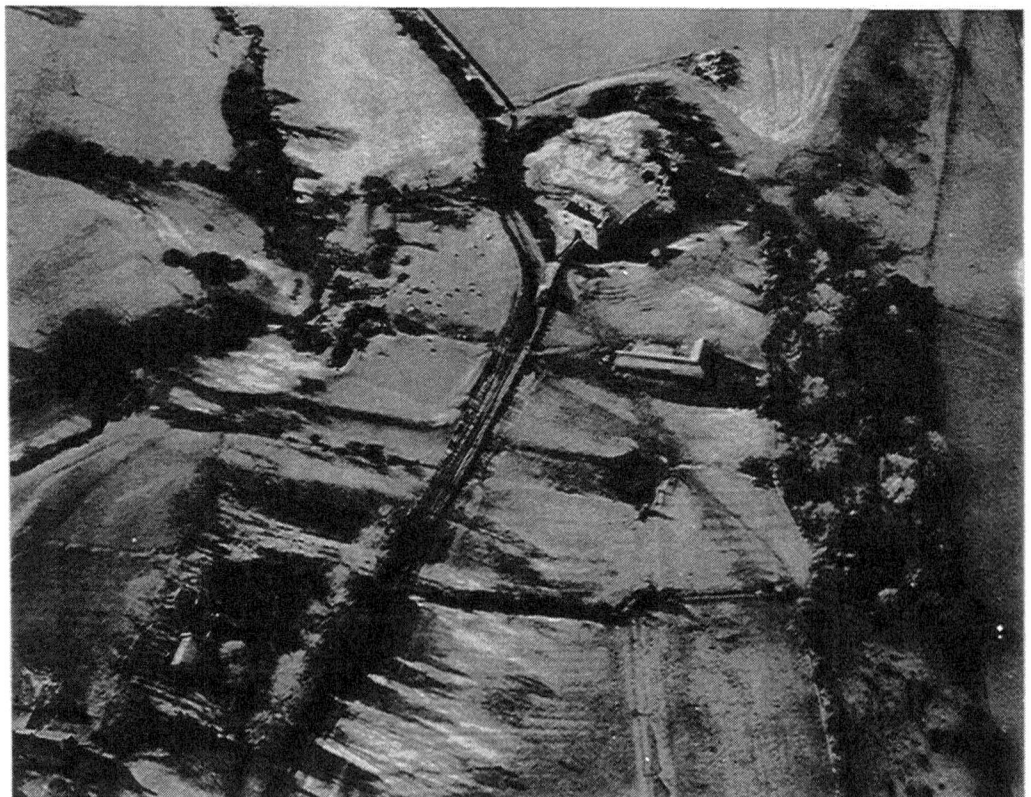

Figure 18
Whorlton Castle, North Yorkshire: air photographic view from the east, 1991 (NMR 12098/20; RCHME © Crown copyright).

an earlier medieval ringwork-and-bailey, prominently sited on an elevated knoll on the northern flank of the North York moors, was adapted in the mid to late 14th century to a residence dressed, like Bodiam, in the emblems of chivalric pretension (NMR No NZ 40 SE 5-8; Mackay and Bowden 1994; Emery 1996, 413-4). What survives through later reuse is principally the three-storey gatehouse block (Corbett 1994). This has an heraldic array over its vaulted entrance passage and such features as a portcullis slot (and presumably portcullis) but no housing for a

34

winch mechanism or other means of raising and lowering such a (literal) fixture. Aligned directly on this gatehouse, and approximately fossilised in the modern by-road that approaches it from Whorlton village to the east, was the access route to the castle. In the dip below the castle the most prominent landscape feature is a large and sharply defined subrectangular pond nearly 200 m long ('a' in Fig 17). It lies at right angles to the road, which divides it unequally in two. These are, in practice, functionally two separate ponds on either side of the road causeway; but their effective coherence, and the complexity and precision of water management entailed in their functioning argue for the planned and ornamental nature of this design. Though we might perhaps contemplate an origin in the 16th-century occupation of the castle when it was refurbished as a country house, the occasion and focus of the arrangement seems to be the 14th-century new work. The enclosed parcels lying with the ponds presumably formed closes, paddocks, orchards, etc in a contemporary layout. This perhaps also included the large enclosed area, extending eastwards within an earthwork boundary, similar in form to a park pale. An early post-medieval park at Whorlton is shown, by contemporary estate maps, to have occupied virtually the whole of the parish north and east of the castle and village, extending to 443 acres (179 hectares). However, field names suggest that there had formerly been a small park of less than 50 acres (20 hectares) on the slopes south west of the castle, on the far side from the ornamental approach, and all on falling ground within its view. An additional possibility is that the present village of Whorlton, which lies to the east slightly away from the parish church and immediately outside the pattern of closes, was shifted to or focused on that location within this overall reordering of the landscape, leaving the church of Holy Cross isolated as the focus of the view from the gatehouse.

Shotwick Castle in Cheshire (Fig 19) is located on the end of a natural spur created by two small, but deep-cut stream valleys, as they empty into the Dee estuary. It had its origin as an early royal castle, evidently of motte-and-bailey form. It, too, experienced a transformation, perhaps similarly in the 14th century, which saw the motte converted (presumably lowered) to become a platform for a polygonal castellated enclosure with towers at the angles and a twin-towered gatehouse at the south-west corner. This is known only from schematic records of its ruins in the 17th century (NMR No SJ 37 SW 6 and 18; Tuck and Jecock 1996). The stream valley on the north west was remodelled to accommodate a network of three principal ponds and by-pass channels. The stream valley on the south side was also altered, albeit less extensively (Fig 20). Such a scale of modification of the natural topography is one of the notable and recurrent aspects of this class of later medieval designed landscapes. The ponds and location of the gatehouse strongly suggest a manipulated approach from the landward side, articulated by the water features. A regular pattern of slight earthworks in the former bailey apparently evidence its conversion into an enclosed garden or herber, of the sort familiar from manuscript illuminations. In this altered guise, Shotwick Castle sat within and formed the functional focus of a late medieval hunting park of 1,000 acres (405 hectares) now administratively fossilised as the extra-parochial township of Shotwick Park. Its distinctive form and embellishments arguably reflect its special role within a landscape of pleasure. Its location on the cliff-like shore of the Dee estuary provided views across to north Wales and a continuing basis for recollection of an earlier, more directly military role that was preserved in its name and in the show of its polygonal, towered curtain and gatehouse occupying the former motte. This architectural form might have continued to evoke royal and military connections by reference to greater castles located across the estuary, as was arguably the case with Holt Castle on the Dee little more than 10 miles (16 km) away (Butler 1987), and with other castles as geographically diverse as Bolingbroke or Goodrich. But, as shown by manuscript illustrations, such forms could also, simultaneously and without contradiction, have other reference points in the discourse of pleasure parks and pleasaunces (for example, Landsberg 1995, 18, 23).

We interpret the changes indicated by the earthworks at Shotwick as relating to a change in function for the castle: with the creation of a hunting park the castle acted as a form of elaborate residence within it. It may be that such elaboration of structure and setting was not uncommon in these circumstances and that a number of field remains, hitherto simply categorised as moats or lodges associated with deer parks, would repay renewed, inquisitive attention. No systematic or synthetic study has yet been undertaken from this standpoint; but, by way of example, Rosemary Hoppitt's doctoral study of the medieval and early post-medieval parks of Suffolk (Hoppitt 1992) affords a number of cases. For example, at Wingfield Castle near Eye and at Pond Hall, Hadleigh, new owners obtained both licence to crenellate and licence to empark (the latter without strict need since they lay far outside any forest area), and were evidently intent on enhancing their new properties with a view to amenity and setting rather than defence. The evidence of any field remains has not yet been assessed in these instances, but the aspiration inherent in obtaining such licences may be a useful marker of residences of this type and a signpost towards future fieldwork. By contrast, work on several standing structures, newly recognised as survivals of park lodges, has re-

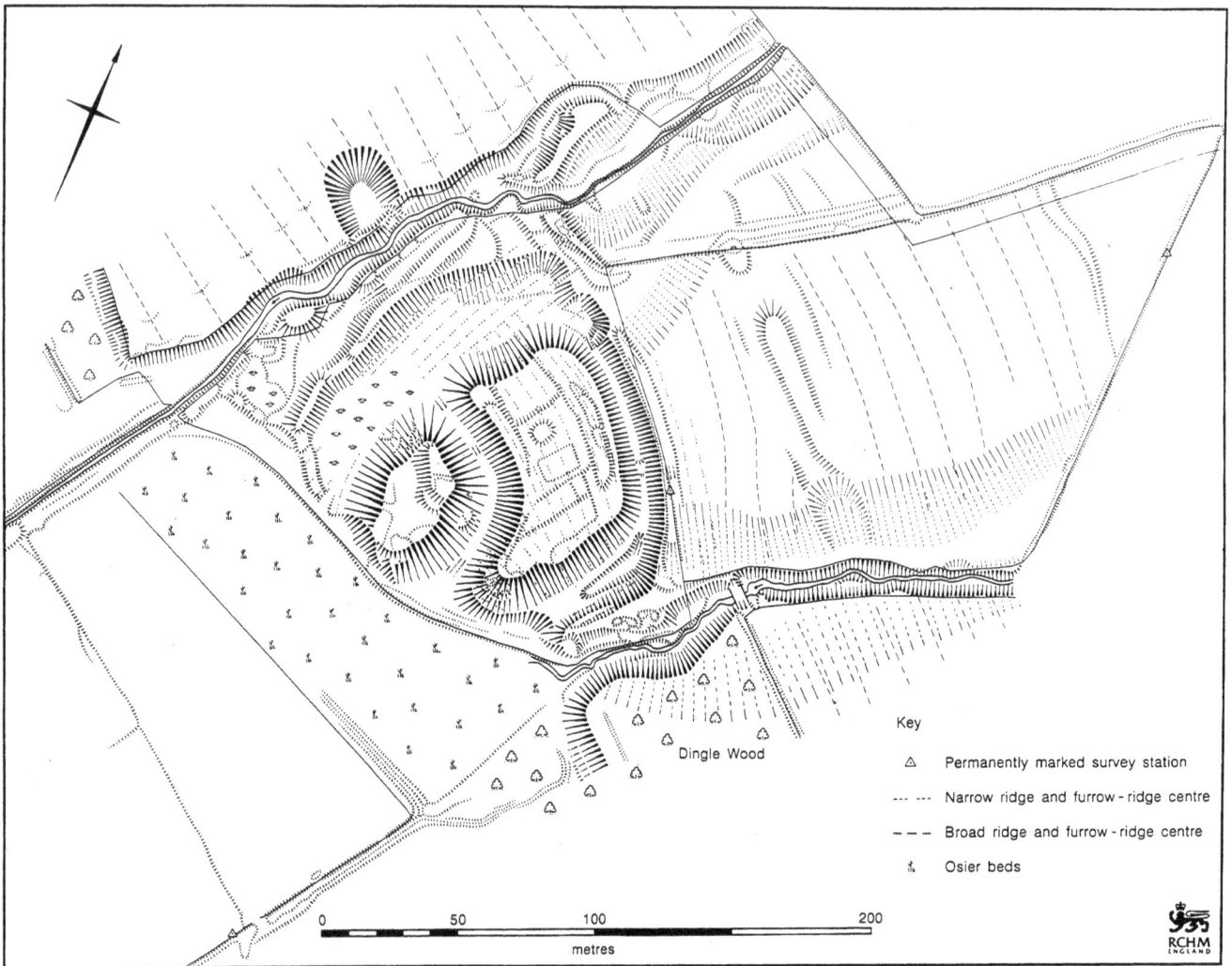

Key

△   Permanently marked survey station

--- ---   Narrow ridge and furrow - ridge centre

– – –   Broad ridge and furrow - ridge centre

⚘   Osier beds

Dingle Wood

0   50   100   200

metres

Figure 19
Shotwick Castle,
Cheshire: survey
plan, original at
1:1 000 scale
(RCHME,
© Crown copyright).

cently clarified both the generally modest form and specific contemporary nomenclature of what can be an unhelpfully loose categorisation of site (Papworth 1994; Roberts 1995, esp 98–103; for the lodge at Harringworth in Northamptonshire see RCHME 1975b, 50–1; RCHME 1984, 87–8). Even then, buildings can be distinctive and of some pretension, as notably at Cranborne in Dorset (RCHME 1975a, 7–12). Earthworks that in themselves suggest contrivance of context and interest in appearance in the landscape include the moated site at Coppenhall Gorse near Stafford, that lies within a park called Hyde Park (NMR SJ 92 SW 43; information from Marcus Jecock, RCHME), and that at Park Farm, Eaton Bray, Bedfordshire (NMR SP 92 SE 4; information from Dave Went, English Heritage), both with their access elaborated by an array of fishponds. The setting of the Prior of Wenlock's 13th-century house and hunting park at Great Oxenbold was enhanced by the adjacent contemporary great fishpool. The house lies parallel with the imposing earthwork of the dam ('a' in Fig 21), forming a grouping viewable advantageously from above, from within the park (NMR No SO 59 SE 8; Wilson-North and Cocroft 1987; Stamper 1996, 8 and Plate 2; mentioned above).

These are confessedly examples at random, but in that very fact may alert us to a substantial phenomenon.

The combination of Whorlton and Shotwick, in addition, may perhaps be taken to exhibit field remains of the three principal elements or types characteristic of medieval gardens in contemporary documents and illustrations (Landsberg 1995, 11–25). These are, an enclosed herber (at Shotwick); an immediate setting of pleasure – the ponds and anonymous closes or paddocks (at both sites, but at Whorlton perhaps extending the length of the aligned approach road and taking in the church site) – and the wider hunting park. In using these characterisations, I deliberately seek to emphasise potential congruence between the field evidence and non-fieldwork studies, notably by John Harvey in documentary evidence and Sylvia Landsberg in recreating early gardens, that have helped to define these typical elements and thereby aid their recognition. In these terms, elements intermediate between the residence and wider park may, quite commonly, be present in the landscape as part of many complexes, as they ought to be. Apparently characterised in contemporary texts as the 'pleasure park' or 'little park' and typically including

36

groves of trees and animal enclosures, they are awkward to document archaeologically, both because they are likely to present themselves as little more than embanked closes, paddocks or existing fields, and because of an absence of accepted nomenclature. Yet these were clearly essential components of designed medieval landscapes, not least in sustaining symbolic imagery. In some cases we may unwittingly already have noted the existence of relevant features, in logging unusually small deer parks. For example, that at Eaton Bray (see above) was only about 28 acres (11 hectares), with an elaborate fishpond known as the 'T' garden at 400–500 m distance from the residence in its secluded western corner. The deer park at Linwood in Lincolnshire, for which ten does and two bucks were granted to stock it in 1252, was not 10 acres (4 hectares) in extent and attached to the manorial court (Everson, Taylor and Dunn 1991, 127–9). This same complex contains, in its second, rectangular 'moat', an earthwork which Christopher Taylor long ago proposed might be a medieval enclosed garden or orchard (1983b plate 17). It is within this context, perhaps, rather than as an enclosed garden, that the earthworks identified as a medieval garden at St Cross, near Winchester, best find a place (Currie 1992); they have the name 'Coneygree' associated with them.

The formerly routine presence of pleasure parks of this sort is perhaps most convincingly seen reflected in a continuing tradition of 16th- and 17th-century examples. One might think of such diverse cases as the small park known as the Coneygree integrated with the garden layout at Chipping Campden (Everson 1989), the brick-walled deer enclosure called Buck Orchard, some 250 m², recently identified at Hoards Park near Bridgnorth (Stamper 1996, 19–20), or the warren focused on the so-called 'Triangular' or Warrener's Lodge at Rushton. The recent elucidation of this particular symbolic landscape, remarkably combining the building and warren earthworks and the rabbit's role (in a tableau vivant) in symbolising the human soul's hope of salvation through the Resurrection (Stocker and Stocker 1996), is a salutory reminder of what we are liable to be missing in interpreting many fieldwork situations. As again the manuscript illustrations repeatedly make clear, most managed animals within medieval garden landscapes might similarly have borne symbolic meaning or emblematic significance, as at Stow Park where I began.

My conclusion is therefore to assert that we have identified examples of medieval gardens and designed landscapes as surviving field remains and can hope to carry that further. It is an exciting area of discovery and new ideas. But to do so we often have to work hard at the field remains; we have at the same time to work hard at an integrated understanding of the buildings

and we have to work hard and imaginatively at the landscape context. But overarching all these, we have to work doubly hard at the cultural context of contemporary belief and image. Since that can be difficult without a specialist background, we have to seek cross-disciplinary co-operation; or, at minimum, as field archaeologists put the field evidence forward in ways that allow its relevance and potential to be recognised by those not concerned with its technical detail (see Taylor this volume).

But really there is a more fundamental conclusion than this. It is that whenever we look at the sites and setting of these great medieval

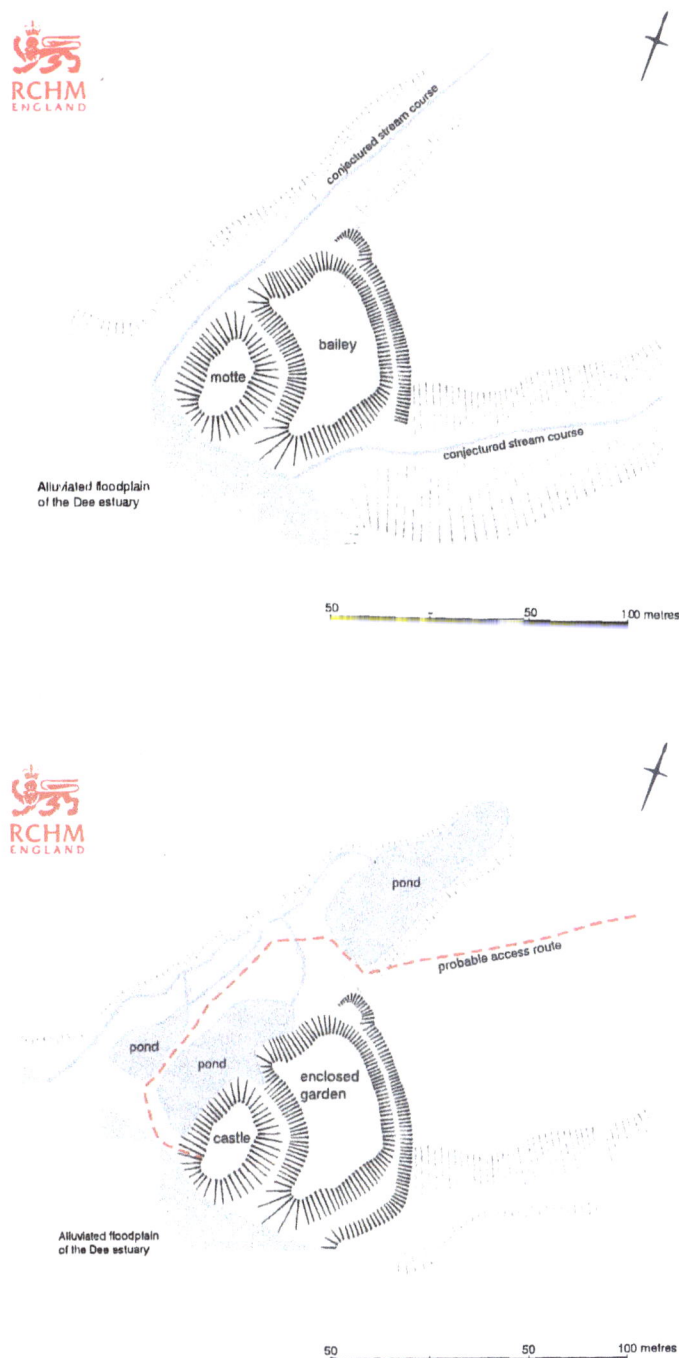

Figure 20
Shotwick Castle, Cheshire: schematic interpretation of the modification of its landscape setting; top, conjectured reconstruction of the topography of the early motte-and-bailey castle; bottom, later medieval castle with its ponds and probable access route (RCHME, © Crown copyright).

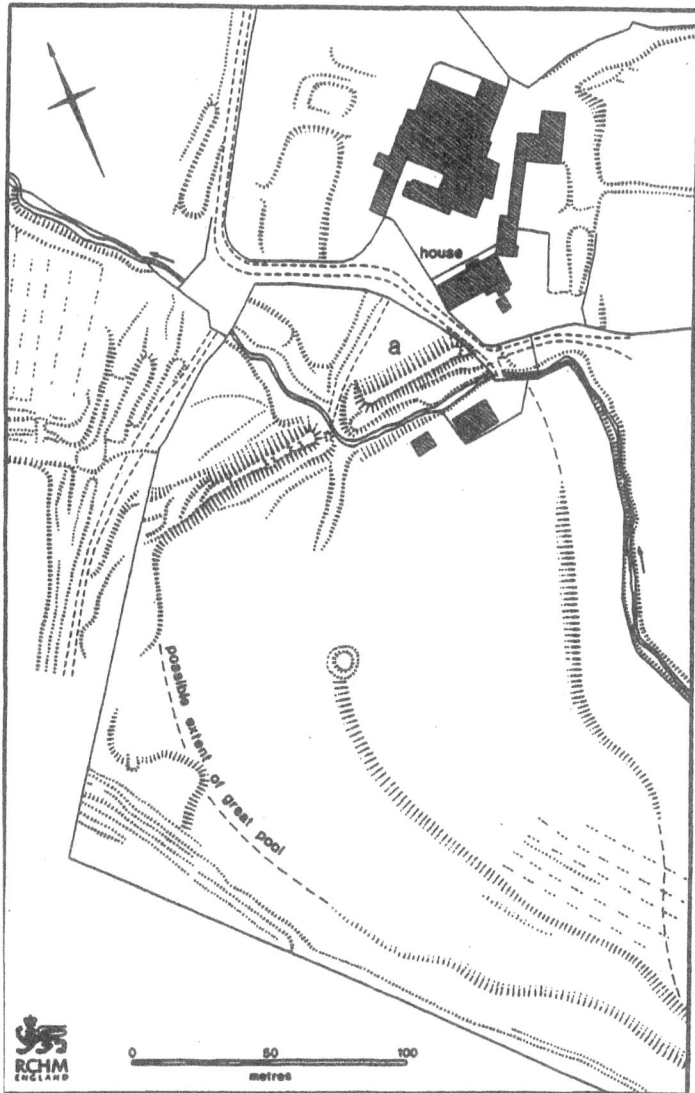

Figure 21
*Great Oxenbold,
Shropshire: survey
plan, original at
1:1 000 scale
(RCHME,
© Crown copyright).*

remains of 'buildings-in-a-landscape', in a way that they rarely are in written documentation, and that need to be recorded and understood.

Among the early responses to the publication of RCHME's work at Bodiam Castle was a letter from Sylvia Landsberg. She quoted from the 12th-century writings of Chrétien de Troyes:

> *Round the garden there was no wall or
> fence, except of air, yet by magic the garden
> was enclosed on every side by air, so that
> nothing could enter it, anymore than if it
> were ringed about by iron, unless it flew over
> the top.*

She noted the consonance, as she felt, between the literary image and the archaeological interpretation at Bodiam. It is such contexts of image and symbolism that are indeed the challenge of medieval gardens for anyone seriously interested in them, and field archaeology should and can make a distinctive contribution to their understanding.

ACKNOWLEDGEMENTS

My colleagues Mark Bowden, Wayne Cocroft, Gary Corbett, Marcus Jecock, Donnie Mackay, Catherine Tuck and Robert Wilson-North carried through the surveys of Shotwick and Whorlton castles and Great Oxenbold that form the core illustrations of this paper. Their hardwork and generosity in making results available underpin it. My debt to friends outside RCHME, who have been equally generous with information, ideas, and the stimulation of shared interest, is no less and extends most directly to Rosemary Hoppitt, Paul Stamper, David Stocker, Christopher Taylor and Dave Went. Philip Sinton and Moraig Brown prepared the illustrations.

The archived plans and site accounts are available for public consultation during normal office hours at the National Monuments Record Centre, Great Western Village, Kemble Drive, Swindon SN2 2GZ; telephone (01793) 414600, fax (01793) 414606.

buildings and there is a body of field evidence surviving to work with, we find that they are part of a carefully manipulated landscape. In contrast to the aesthetic content of parks and gardens of the 18th century and later, it is unclear that any are purely or predominantly aesthetic, which is a later concept. They are, in one way or another, symbolic, reflecting concerns that are always present. These concerns are embedded in the field

GIANT STEPS: FIELDWORK IN LONDON'S ROYAL PARKS

Paul Pattison

ABSTRACT

The Royal Parks of Greater London present a variety of landscapes from the most urban and obviously designed Regents Park to the more rural wood-pasture of Richmond. Yet all of them started life as rural parks and have survived, largely intact, as London slowly, then rapidly encircled them. From around the time of James I, they gradually changed from places open only to the elite to ones of public recreation and entertainment, but despite this they have retained a royal connection. As protected open areas the Royal Parks preserve information about the constant development which they have undergone in the form of buildings, landscape, planting and earthworks. Until recently they had remained largely unexplored by archaeologists.

The RCHME has carried out selective field surveys in all those parks administered by the Royal Parks Agency, plus the former park at Nonsuch in Surrey. It has revealed a rich variety of archaeological features which complement the extensive historical information summarised so admirably in the Land Use Consultants reports of the 1980s. This paper will examine, only briefly, a few aspects of those field surveys undertaken in five parks: Hyde, Greenwich, Richmond, Bushy and Nonsuch. It can only give a fleeting glimpse of what has been revealed.

THE ORIGIN OF THE ROYAL PARKS AS WORKING LANDSCAPES

All the parks were originally working landscapes, starting life as private reserves; securely enclosed areas where deer and other animals were kept for many varieties of hunting; they were also open-air larders – great food sources to be drawn on when needed. However, we should not forget that parks were of additional economic value in the provision of various other natural resources: pasture for domestic beasts, underwood for the fire and precious timber for building, and even for small-scale industrial purposes. For instance,

a map of 1675 – the so-called *Pepys' Plan* (Magdalene College, Cambridge) – revealed that gravel was extracted in Greenwich Park before the Restoration and it has left a permanent mark on the distinctive undulating topography. There were similar gravel pits in Hyde Park, one of which was adapted by George London and Henry Wise into a sunken Wilderness garden for Queen Anne in the early 18th century (Land Use Consultants 1982a, 9) and another, by the Serpentine, is now the tree-lined dell called The Cockpit.

The enclosure of the parks, often on manorial waste, marginal or common land, where local people had customary rights, was not always done by agreement and caused resentment. In 1433, Duke Humphrey of Gloucester's enclosure of the park at Greenwich – the oldest Royal Park – involved the diversion of a public road and loss of common land on Blackheath. Henry VIII – the prolific park-maker – who was largely responsible for the creation of the Royal Parks, took similar liberties. In the later stages of his reign, wanting to be able to hunt close to London, he created St James in 1532, Hyde in 1536 and Regent's in 1540. His creation of Nonsuch Palace and Park towards the end of his life involved the demolition of an entire village at Cuddington, including its church and manor house, some details of which were found by Martin Biddle's excavations in 1959–60 (Colvin 1982, 179; Dent 1981, 239–58). Between 1619 and 1624, James I's building of a brick wall around the park at Greenwich involved modification to the older course of the park pale; land was appropriated and forced the following plea from a dispossessed resident:

> *...a field of arable ground, 10 acres, in the occupation of John Morten otherwise John Gardener, upon the King's Majesty enclosing with a brick wall his Park, he took a great portion of these 10 acres and of common towards the River, whereupon I petitioned him but never got anything for the loss. God turne his Harte* (Fear 1961–3, 8–13)

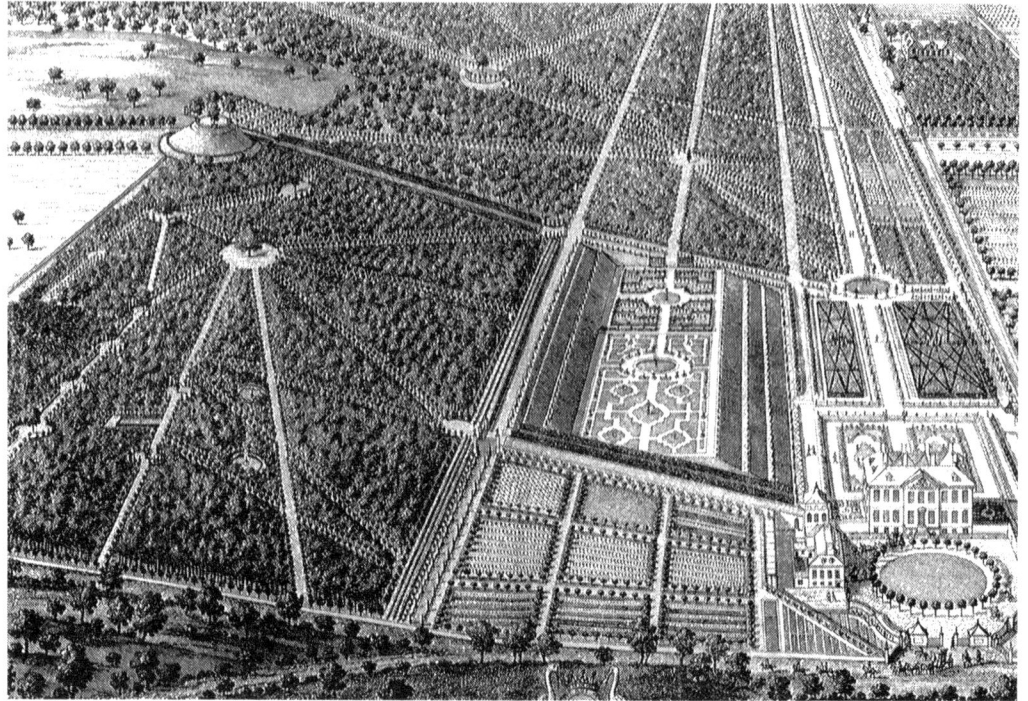

Figure 22
*Richmond Park, Greater
London: New Park
(Petersham Park): the
elaborate formal gardens
around 1700 showing
Henry VIII's Mound at
top left (Knyff and Kip
1707, fig 33).*

As late as 1637, the forcible creation of Richmond Park was opposed and bitterly resented.

The Royal Parks vary in size but tend to the larger of medieval parks which were generally quite small – 100–200 acres (40–80 ha) (Steane 1993, 148) – and not big areas for the full-blooded chase. Consequently, hunting in parks became highly ritualised and carefully planned. By Tudor times a common method of hunting in parks was the killing of driven game: the whole affair was carefully planned – the quarry was located beforehand, then during the hunt it was driven by horses and dogs, sometimes between a series of stations where fresh horses and dogs could be taken. Finally, it was driven into a natural killing ground or past a standing where hunters waited with bow or gun and spectators paraded in their finery (Lasdun 1991, 17–18; Steane 1993, 150–2). By their nature standings were often of a temporary nature and are not well known. In Richmond Park, however, an earthen mound known in 1637 as 'the Kinges Standing' (PRO: map of the New Parke, Richmond, Surrey by Elias Allen) and later given its present name, Henry VIII's Mound, almost certainly functioned in this way. It lay at the southern end of a tree-lined avenue (Fig 22), at the northern end of which was another artificial mound, Olivers Mount, shown on John Rocque's plan of 1741–5. Could this be a hunting course enshrined in planting?

In Nonsuch Park the banqueting house built for Henry VIII, around 1540, stood at the centre of a raised ornamental platform which may have functioned as a standing. The two-storeyed building had large windows and, at each of its four corners, a 'balcone placed for prospect'

(Colvin 1982, 202), possibly in part for watching the hunt.

Tom Greeves' work in Richmond and Bushy revealed that substantial areas contained, not only information about their development as parklands, but also about their pre-enclosure landscapes (Greeves 1992; 1993). In Richmond, for instance, on the steep escarpment overlooking the Thames Valley, several earthen mounds were identified which might be of prehistoric origin. Two of them are thought by Greeves to be candidates for Neolithic long barrows – the communal tombs of the first farming communities in these islands. In Richmond also, the 17th-century enclosure extinguished chunks of the landuse patterns of several surrounding parishes: the redundant field boundaries and cultivation remains of the late medieval period can still be traced and it remains a priority to map and analyse this multi-period landscape accurately. Similar large tracts of late medieval landscape are preserved in Bushy Park and there are even fragments in Hyde Park, revealed initially by studying air photographs, and subsequently by careful survey on the ground. Here, there are slight traces of fields and arable agriculture, associated with the manor of Hyde, from which the park was formed in 1536 (RCHME 1994; NMR No TQ 28 SE 165).

NONSUCH PARK

Sometimes, survey reveals the opposite of what is expected (RCHME 1995). In Nonsuch Park, far from revealing the anticipated remains of a medieval landscape – Cuddington's fields before Henry VIII swept them away for the construction of his new palace and gardens – there emerged a pattern which began in the late 17th century, after the sale and demolition of the palace, when the entire park was given over to agricultural land and largely ploughed. The subtle earthwork banks and ridge and furrow revealed were of 18th-century origin, not medieval, an observation only made possible by ground survey and documentary study in close combination. As John Phibbs points out (this volume), it is all too easy to make assumptions about cultivation remains in parkland.

Although the Tudor palace of Nonsuch has been explored by excavation, its gardens are known largely from documents. It was a relatively small palace intended only for the riding household and not the full court, but it is unique in that both palace and gardens were designed and built in a single episode – a rare occurrence in England – utilising the most up-to-date thinking of the time. Something of its magnificence is shown by Speed's illustration of 1610. The survey plan (Fig 23) reveals that two of the post-demolition fields preserve the principal plan elements of the palace and its gardens: two large precisely square compartments, each side measuring 180m . One contained the palace, notably located centrally to one axis and approached along an axial avenue from the north. The palace compartment was sub-divided by walls into kitchen garden, orchard and privy garden, some details of which are known. The layout of the second compartment, called the Wilderness, is more enigmatic but its square plan probably meant that it was further divided into squares. However, documentary sources record three walks, perhaps central and flanking as at Hampton Court: a low raised bank located during survey along the western and southern sides may be a remnant of one.

Documents also record a grotto, the 'Grove of Diana', which was particularly appropriate to a hunting park. This was probably built after the Ridolphi Plot of 1571, as an apology to Elizabeth I by the then owner, Henry Fitzalan, a fallen favourite of the queen (Martin Biddle pers comm). Its centrepiece was a statuary group depicting the myth of Actaeon being run down by his own hounds, perhaps an allegorical reference to the relationship between Fitzalan and Elizabeth. The precise location of the grotto is unknown and has been taken to be a field immediately west of the Wilderness. However, located against the Wilderness boundary and central to its axis, is a looping earthwork located at a drop in ground level – a very suitable site for a grotto (Dent 1981, 121; RCHME 1995, 13–14).

The banqueting house at Nonsuch stood in open ground on a high point in the park, but only a few hundred metres away from the palace. Its ornamental platform appears to be playfully modelled on Camber Castle, one of the Henrician artillery forts on the Kent coast built after 1540 (Colvin 1982, 202). The building fulfilled several functions: perhaps with its mock military artillery bastions it was a symbolic sentinel for the palace, it was a private retreat where light refreshment could be taken and from its viewing gallery a prospect of the palace and its gardens would be visible, as would the progress of the hunt. As we have seen, the platform may also have functioned as a standing.

Nonsuch Park has been progressively eroded by housing encroachment and there is pressure still: recent developments have taken place in the south of the park and there is the possibility of more. Yet there is enormous potential for garden history here: an entire Tudor garden complex survives relatively undisturbed and uncluttered

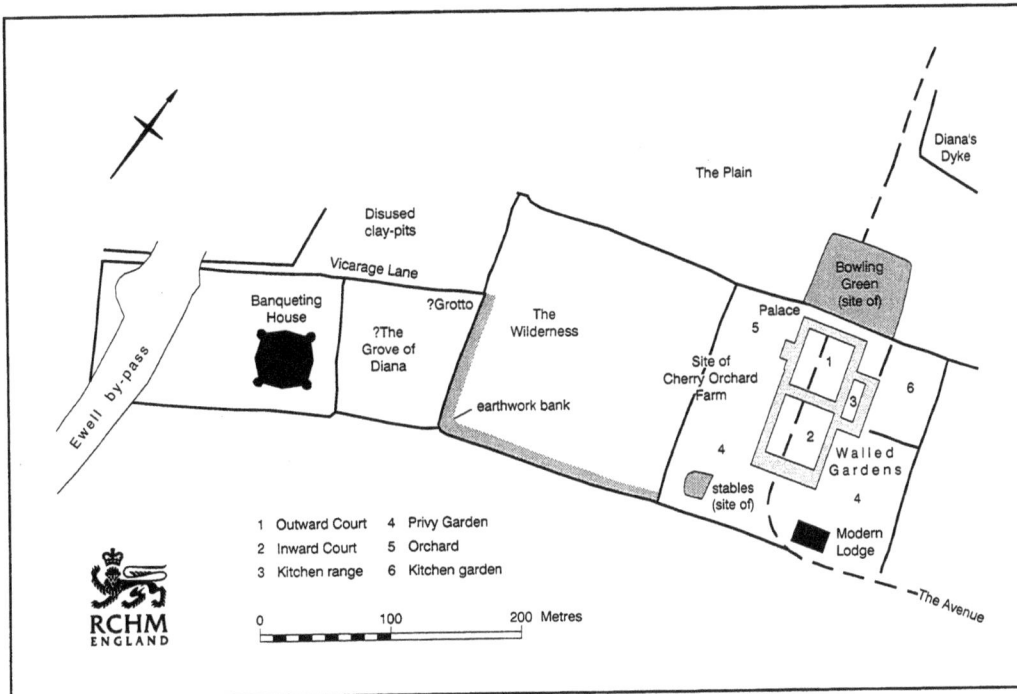

Figure 23
Nonsuch Park, Greater London: interpretation plan showing the conjectured layout of the Tudor gardens (RCHME, © Crown copyright).

by subsequent development since its dismantling towards the end of the 17th century. We should be careful to protect it.

GREENWICH PARK

Greenwich Park is a rectangular area stretching from low ground near the Thames, the site of the royal palace, up and across the line of a steep escarpment and onto the plateau, south of Blackheath. Within the Park the RCHME recorded seventy-six surface features, ranging from a Romano-British temple site to the faint traces of air-raid shelters and barrage balloon emplacements from the Second World War (RCHME 1994a). There was considerable evidence of small-scale gravel quarrying, ranging in date

from before 1660 to the 19th century, in the form of pits and cuts, which in places has given additional sharpness to the naturally convoluted topography.

A remarkable survival are the burial mounds, sitting unobtrusively in open parkland; a cemetery of thirty-one small circular barrows, no greater than 10 m across and 1 m high. In 1784, twenty of them were explored by the Reverend James Douglas, a notable antiquary and pioneer in the study of Anglo-Saxon burial. He found that each mound covered a single primary inhumation burial, placed in a grave cut into the old ground surface. In eight graves there were simple grave goods: two with iron spearheads and others with an iron knife, a shield boss and small glass beads (Douglas 1793, 89–91). These finds are

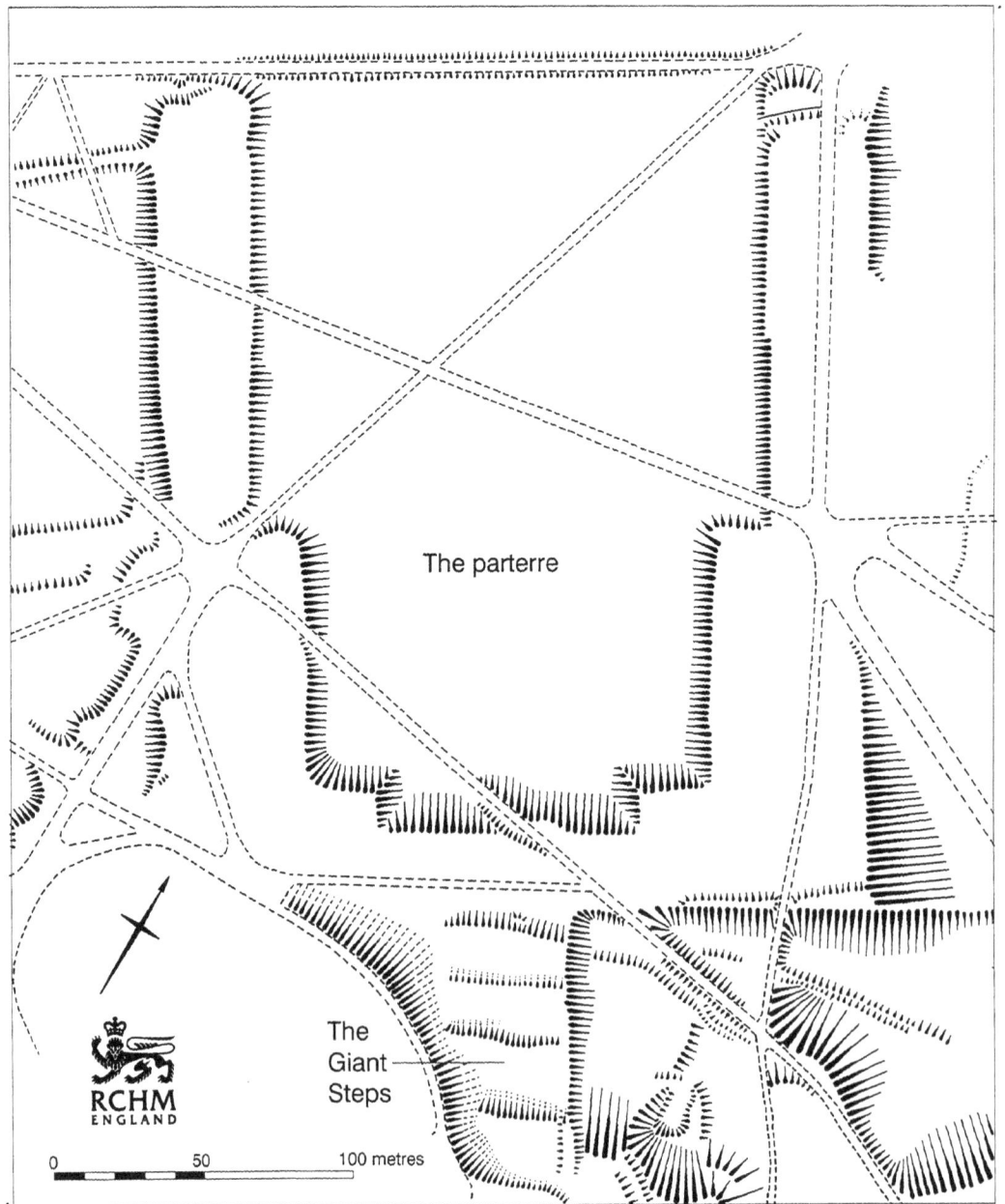

The parterre

The Giant Steps

RCHM ENGLAND

0   50   100 metres

*Figure 24
Greenwich Park, Greater London: survey plan of the earthworks of an unfinished parterre, designed by André le Nôtre (RCHME, © Crown copyright).*

typically Anglo-Saxon and were deposited sometime between the 6th and 8th centuries AD.

The survival of such ephemeral features is undoubtedly due to enclosure of the park, and beforehand, the unsuitability of the soils here for arable agriculture. Nevertheless, it is likely that these burial mounds were deliberately respected as ancient features, and therefore largely unaffected by planting. Similarly, a mound marking the site of a Roman temple in the park survived, in this case utilised as the culmination of one of the Restoration avenues, and planted with a circle of elms.

However, perhaps of greatest interest are the events immediately following the Restoration in 1660, involving changes which have left the most obvious and lasting impact on the park. The king's plans for Greenwich involved the demolition of the old Tudor buildings, the repair and enlarging of the Queen's House and the construction of a massive new palace between it and the river. The project was abandoned in 1669 with the palace incomplete, but the implementation of a formal layout for the Park, to complement the planned palace, was much further advanced. The origin of this design is unkown but its details reveal continental influence. More-or-less contemporary replanning in St James Park was assisted by several Frenchmen including the brothers Mollet and it is possible that they, too, advised on Greenwich (Strong 1992,10–12): one of their typical devices, the *pate d'oie*, was present in both parks. The plan for Greenwich was a formal layout of tree-lined walks: a main axis south east from Queen's House, up the escarpment via a series of massive turf steps called *Ascents* (later the *Giant Steps*) and on to Blackheath. There were two main cross avenues, a *pate d'oie* at the southern end, running diagonally north and north west and further diagonal avenues between the cross avenues. Across the southern end, rectangular blocks of coppice woodland, *The Wildernesses*, divided by walks, extended to the park boundaries.

Works in Greenwich Park began in the autumn of 1661, when seven of the major avenues, the *Wilderness* plantations and the *Giant Steps* were laid out. All were completed by June 1662. In May 1662, the king asked Loius XIV for the assistance of his garden designer André le Nôtre. From a surviving sketch, with notes in le Nôtre's hand, we know that he provided a plan for a large parterre on the low ground between Queen's House and the Giant Steps. The RCHME survey illustrates how the framework provided by this plan was implemented (Fig 24): the parterre earthworks were cut into the foot of the escarpment and spoil was shaped into massive earthen banks on the flanks of the planned garden, the gentle slope of which was carefully graded. The proportions are almost exactly as designed. Some of the steps, badly eroded, can still be discerned, especially in the low-angled light of winter sunshine.

The plan of Greenwich has nothing like the carefully orchestrated overall unity and symmetry of contemporary French gardens. It is in fact strongly asymmetrical, partly because of existing constraints: the natural combes, the irregular shape of the Park wall and the off-centre axis dictated by Queen's House. The striking element of Greenwich was and is the fusion between the natural topography and the artificial layout of its avenues. The formal element found its focus on the huge baroque ensemble of Greenwich Hospital, but despite this, Greenwich retained something of its medieval parkland character, and did not become a formal garden.

HYDE PARK AND KENSINGTON GARDENS

Large-scale landscape design also took place in Hyde Park. From the 1630s, limited public access was permitted and the emphasis in the park shifted towards ornament and display, stimulated by the establishment of a circular carriage track and racecourse in the centre of the eastern side of the Park. Known as the 'Tour' or the 'Ring', it became a fashionable parade for high society until the 1730s (Land Use Consultants 1982a, 9–11). Today, slight traces remain in the earthworks and planting.

The major development of Hyde Park, however, had to wait until shortly after the accession of William and Mary. In 1689 they acquired Nottingham House and began its conversion into Kensington Palace, including work on the gardens. Subsequently, under Queen Anne and Queen Caroline the gardens were massively enlarged, with new formal gardens stretching away north and south to the park margins. Development continued until 1737 by which time a huge amount of land had been appropriated from Hyde Park, initially for a menagerie but ultimately for formal gardens, including the creation of the Serpentine (the present area of Hyde Park at 344 acres (139 hectares) is only 55% of the 621 acres (251 hectares) recorded at its sale in 1652). The final enlargement took in higher ground called Buck Hill, creating a long elevated vista back to the palace. This area is presently an open one of close-mown grass, but visibly undulating and disturbed by successive phases of tree planting and removal, and by the ravages of activity here in the Second World War (RCHME 1994b). The RCHME survey of this area revealed the earthworks which defined the eastern edge of Kensington Gardens as completed by 1737. An ornamental ha-ha in a mock military style – designed by Charles Bridgeman – was still definable as a low bank and infilled ditch, as were the outlines of some other elements of the Bridgemanic design (Fig 25).

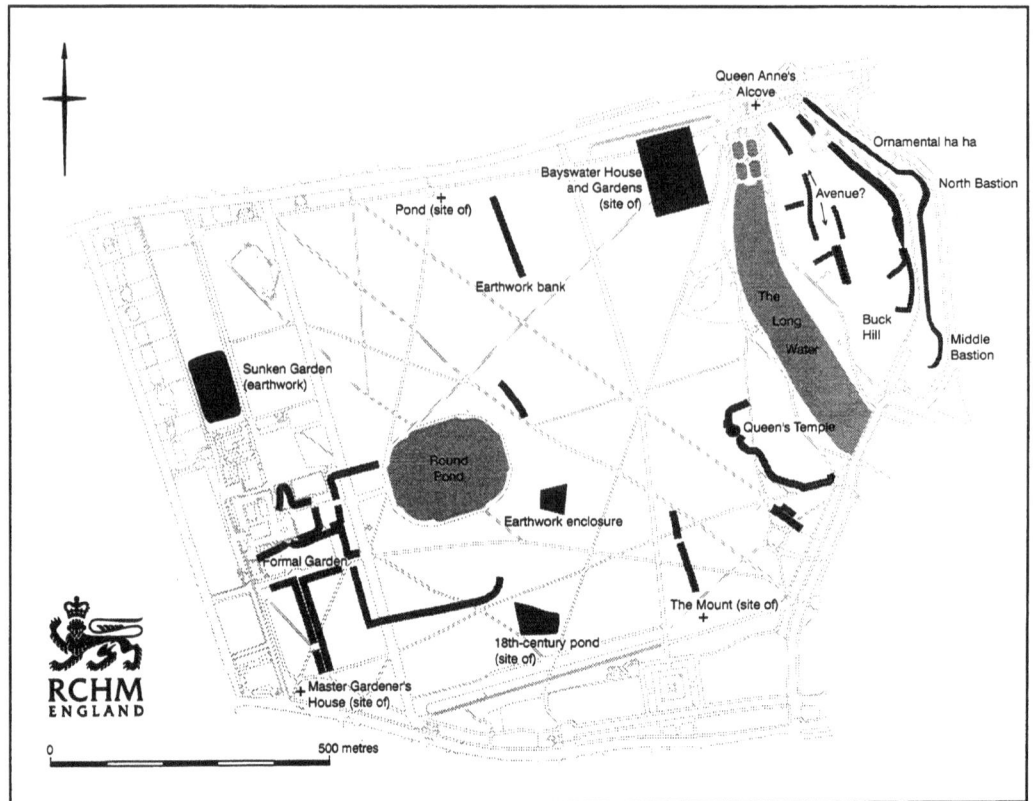

Figure 25
*Kensington Gardens,
Greater London:
interpretation plan
showing surviving
earthwork elements of
the late 17th and early
18th-century gardens.
(RCHME, © Crown
copyright).*

The planted quarters with serpentine paths and planting, which Bridgeman eventually created between the geometric avenues of Kensington Gardens, have long since gone, but one of the buildings which William Kent provided has survived. Queen's Temple is a secluded pavilion designed to be glimpsed between clumps of trees from across the Serpentine, a view now obscured (Strong 1992, 43), but it is still framed by planting, with open ground towards the Serpentine. The building was elevated by siting on a low earthen mound and the slope from it, towards the water, deliberately graded. It remains a fine example of the integration in the siting of a building in an altered landscape, to create a contrived picture.

RICHMOND PARK

In Richmond and Bushy Parks survey activity was confined to selected sites: the areas were simply too large to record in the time available. However, sufficient was observed to state that detailed analyses of both landscapes will reveal a wealth of information about their development.

In Richmond, the survey examined an area formerly known as Petersham Park. On the edge of this area, King Henry VIII's Mound is situated on the brink of a steep westward slope down to the River Thames, with fine prospects in all directions. It was incorporated as a mount in the gardens created by the Earl of Rochester in the late 17th century, during his transformation of Petersham Lodge into a fine house and elaborate

formal garden, as depicted on the perspective drawing by Knyff and Kip (Fig 22; Jacques and van der Horst 1988, 76). The garden occupied an area lying mainly on the steep west-facing slope and along a relatively narrow level strip at its foot. At the back of the house, arranged in series, were elaborate formal compartments, all ordered on and around a central avenue. The unusual element of the design was in the treatment of the steep hillside, which included a massively terraced platform with a double parterre and fountains. But particularly notable was an extensive wooded garden divided into sections, by an interlocking series of *allées*, containing *rond-points* with fountains and large pollards.

To look at this area today, it is almost impossible to believe the former extent and elaboration of these gardens. Yet there can be little doubt of their existence, nor of their intricate nature, given a description in a letter of Samuel Molyneux, dated 14 February 1713 (Dixon-Hunt and Willis 1988, 148–50). Yet by 1834–5 the whole lot had gone, in this case truly 'swept away' and the area returned to Richmond Park. There must have been considerable effort in the landscaping and felling to conceal, almost totally, the terracing and *allées* on the hillside. Survey here was very difficult, exacerbated by the natural slippage of soil deposits and spring-sapping on the hillside. It did, however, reveal slight remains of the garden (Fig 26): the present trackway occupies the central avenue leading south from Petersham Lodge. East of the trackway, and aligned with it, are two parallel linear scarps set 5 m to 7 m apart, forming a terrace which is still flanked by

44

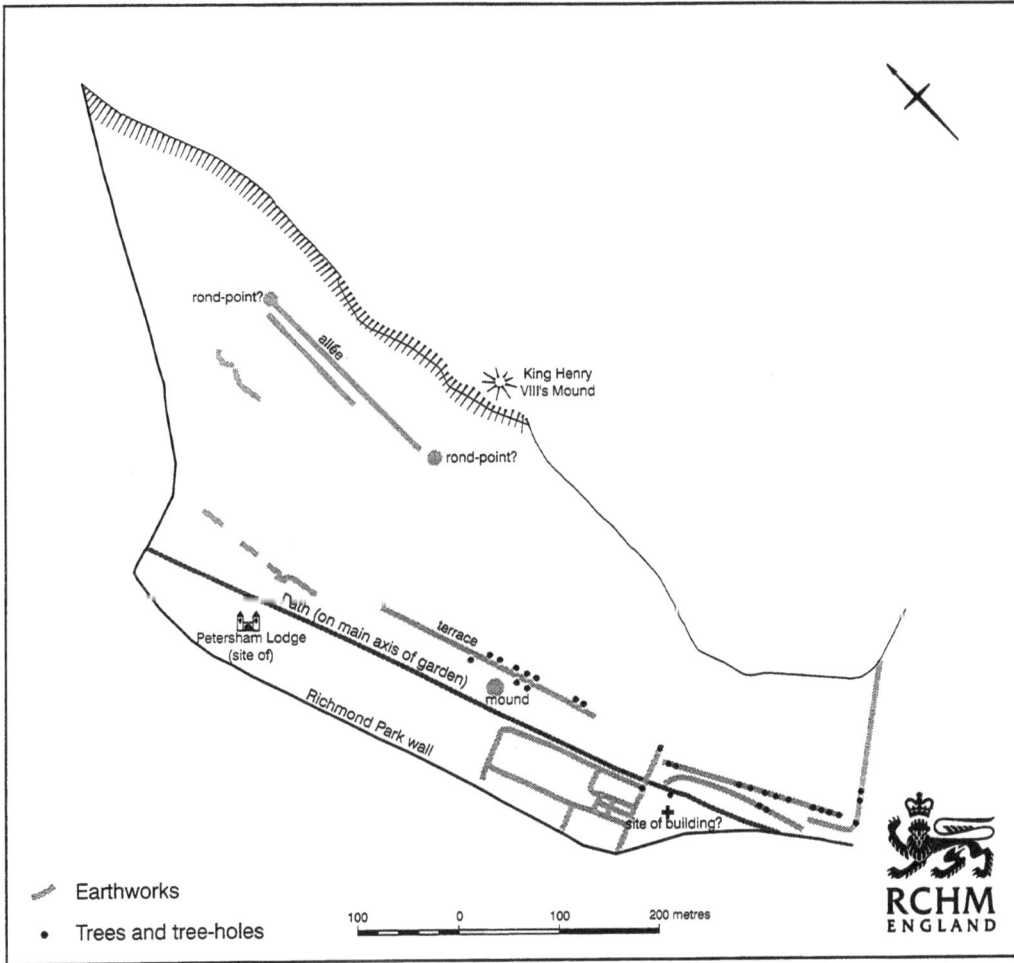

Figure 26
Richmond Park, Greater London: interpretation plan, showing surviving earthworks of the late 17th–18th century garden (RCHME, © Crown copyright).

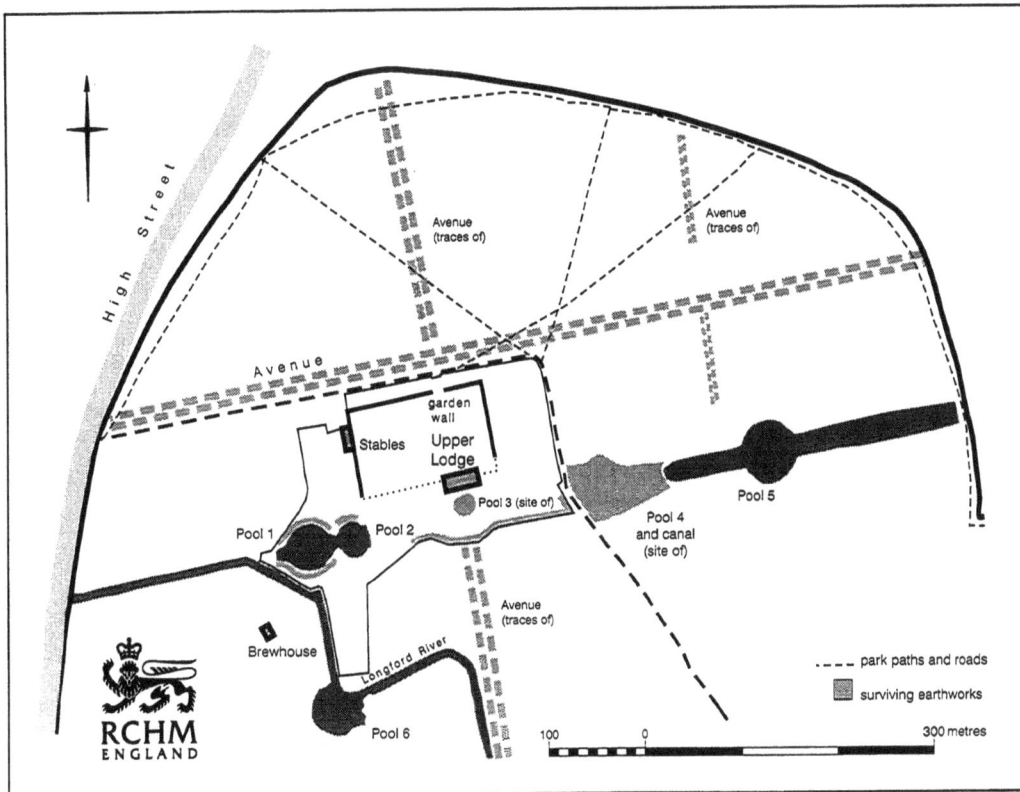

Figure 27
Upper Lodge, Bushy Park, Greater London: interpretation plan showing the surviving elements of the 18th-century water garden and park layout (RCHME, © Crown copyright).

mature trees or pocked by the holes of fallen ones. This is one of the *allées* in the Knyff and Kip perspective, which separated two wooded quarters. Further south towards Sudbrook Park, there are clearer remains of a garden compartment laid out immediately west of the central avenue, comprising a level rectangular area 158 m by 74 m, defined by earthworks. Slight earthworks inside the compartment correspond with the details shown on the Knyff and Kip perspective, a testimony to the reliability of their drawings.

BUSHY PARK

In Bushy Park, survey was limited to two garden sites, Bushy House and Upper Lodge. At the latter site, despite many years of development as the Admiralty Research Laboratory, with the consequent clutter of roads, hard standing and research buildings, the principal elements of a notable garden remain. The house, much altered, is unremarkable, but it goes with fine brick garden walls of the late 17th century and, more importantly, an early 18th-century water garden along its south face. Water from several sources including the Longford river, an artificial watercourse created to supply Hampton Court, was diverted into a long canal and a series of ponds along the south front of the house and through the park. A low cascade was created between two of the ponds, depicted by Stephen Switzer in 1729 and on a painting by the Hungarian artist Jacob Bogdani (in private possession). Much of the framework and most of the canal survives (Fig 27) – as well as the cascade between the two upper pools – and is being promoted for restoration by the Friends of Bushy and Home Parks. This restoration will be founded on a detailed, multi-disciplinary approach within which archaeology will play a pivotal role.

CONCLUSIONS

Although much had been written about the history and development of the Royal Parks, to-wards the end of the 1980s there remained still a big gap in accessible, recorded information on what survived of the visible archaeology. That gap is now not so big: the core of it is available in the National Monuments Record.

It is important to bring this survey information to the attention of all concerned, especially in such important landscapes where archaeology has not been as closely integrated with general park planning as it ought to be. After all, in the Royal Parks where everything down to lamp-stands and rubbish bins is recorded, detailed archaeological survey and an understanding of what might lie under the ground, should be essential elements of management and planning.

Our understanding of parks and gardens can be radically changed by accurate field observation and intelligent interpretation in combination with a growing knowledge of garden history, as has been demonstrated over the past few years in the field of medieval 'designed landscapes' (Everson this volume). Only through such integration will we understand better what we see and make informed decisions about what is important and what to preserve. In many cases, this is happening, more perhaps than was suggested in the opening paper to this conference (Taylor this volume). Nevertheless, we should continue to take such small practical steps forward if we are to achieve any giant ones in our perception of historic parks and gardens.

ACKNOWLEDGEMENTS

I would like to give special thanks to the team who worked on the Royal Parks Project: Al Oswald, Jane Kenny, Paul Struth, Moraig Brown, Trevor Pearson, Peter Topping and Una Sanderson.

The archived plans and site accounts are available for public consultation during normal office hours at the National Monuments Record Centre, Great Western Village, Kemble Drive, Swindon SN2 2GZ; telephone (01793) 414600, fax (01793) 414606.

18TH-CENTURY LANDSCAPES IN NORFOLK, ENGLAND

Tom Williamson

ABSTRACT

For the past seven years the Centre of East Anglian Studies at the University of East Anglia has been undertaking a comprehensive programme of fieldwork and documentary research in an attempt to elucidate the development of designed landscapes in Norfolk and, latterly, Suffolk. This work has concentrated on the period c 1650–1850, although gardens of earlier and later dates have also been examined. This paper will briefly describe some of the methodological and theoretical problems involved in this work, showing the extent to which field survey can greatly extend our knowledge of the development of garden design. In so doing I will present some of our most important results.

INTRODUCTION

The Norfolk Parks and Gardens Survey was started at the centre of East Anglian Studies in the University of East Anglia in 1988, and its final results are currently in press (Williamson in press). What follows is a brief discussion of some of the project's principal findings. I shall limit myself here to what the survey has told us about the development of landscape design in the 18th century, and in particular to the part played by archaeology in this programme of research.

The core of the project was a survey of eighty-five parks and gardens in Norfolk. This was conducted in a variety of ways, by a variety of different people: paid researchers, students, voluntary helpers and a Manpower Services Commission team. It was *not* primarily an archaeological survey, and no attempt was made to plan every earthwork or standing structure encountered. The presence and form of all such features were briefly recorded, together with the essential characteristics of the surviving planting: detailed surveys were made of particular features; and considerable use was made of aerial photography (in association with Derek Edwards of Norfolk Landscape Archaeology). Neverthe-

less, the project was primarily an exercise in 'documentary archaeology' (Beaudry 1993), based on the systematic examination of all maps, documents and illustrations relating to the sample sites. This work, moreover, was accompanied by a more general survey of documentary, cartographic and illustrative material relating to the development of garden design in Norfolk, including a complete examination of every map surveyed before 1800 held by the Norfolk Record Office; a systematic examination of all the family and estate papers held in the Major and Minor Collections in the same repository; and an analysis of contemporary local newspapers. Our intention was to examine a number of specific and related questions concerning the history of designed landscapes in the period up to *c* 1850 and, in particular, to consider the history of gardens within its wider context, by looking at a large sample within a region in which, through other research projects, more general aspects of social and economic history are tolerably well understood.

It is important to distinguish at the outset between the contribution made by a mass, multi-source survey on the one hand; and that made by a specifically archaeological approach on the other. I will begin with the former, before looking briefly at the latter.

SYSTEMATIC SURVEY AND GARDEN HISTORY

The main benefit of surveys of this kind is, quite simply, that they allow us to see the history of gardens, as opposed to the published ideas of fashionable 18th-century writers about the history of gardens. Or, to put it another way, such a study demonstrates forcibly that Garden History, and the History of Gardens, are distinct (though related) *discourses*. Many readers will be fully aware of this notion, even if they do not articulate it in this particular fashion. The account of 18th-century garden history presented by writers like

Horace Walpole is misleading, because it was principally an account of developments taking place at the most fashionable – and often the wealthiest – sites. It is, in this context, useful to make a broad distinction between the local gentry – the squires, men whose estates embraced a parish or two and who had social horizons to match – and the much smaller elite of great landowners. These were men with estates covering 5,000 acres (2,023 hectares) or more and whose social contacts and political activities extended, in many cases, far beyond the bounds of the county. Not all these people were necessarily doing the same things, at the same time. They had different interests, resources and needs: their designed landscapes were, therefore, intended to perform different functions. Nevertheless, in most periods, their grounds normally shared a number of features and it is evident that, even at elite social levels, garden design did not always develop in quite the way, or with quite the pace, that contemporary commentators often seem to suggest.

Indeed, one of the most striking results of the Norfolk survey is its demonstration that, at least in provincial areas of England away from London, the geometric tradition of garden design was very long-lived. Walpole's famous description of the transition from 'geometric' to 'naturalistic' forms gives the impression that the former went into sharp decline following the development of the ha-ha by William Kent in the 1730s (Walpole 1982, 263–4). Many art-historians have detected the seeds of the revolt against formality earlier, in the first three decades of the century (Hadfield 1960; Hussey 1967). In fact, systematic survey suggests that during the first half of the 18th century, in this region at least, garden design at all social levels remained for the most part strongly formal and geometric in style. This does not mean that design was static. On the contrary: the geometric style continued to develop and evolve in this period. At the highest social levels the first three decades of the century saw the replacement of gardens dominated by parterres set in walled enclosures by simpler designs whose principal elements were grass platts, clipped hedges, and ornamental woods or 'wildernesses' (Taigel and Williamson 1991, 11–13). In the 1720s and 30s, perimeter walls began to be replaced by substantial ha-has, and the experience of the deer park and garden were thereby progressively integrated. The period c 1730–60 saw further changes, again largely restricted to the highest social levels. At Houghton, Wolterton and elsewhere, partly under the influence of Charles Bridgeman, the outlines of the geometric garden were simplified still further and projected outwards into the parkland in the form of formal vistas, block planting and avenues. The distinction between the park and garden was thus further dissolved.

The 1730s and 40s are often characterised as a period in which, under the influence of William Kent, more irregular and serpentine forms began to appear in garden designs. Serpentine features were sometimes included in the grounds of Norfolk's elite – serpentine paths within wildernesses, serpentine watercourses – but to a limited extent, and only at one site, Holkham, was a fully-developed 'Italianate' landscape, designed by Kent himself, created (Fig 28). Even this, it should be noted, was slotted into what otherwise remained an essentially geometric design, as was the case at other similar sites in England (Phibbs 1993).

Some sense of this combination of the serpentine and geometric is provided by an advertisement which appeared in the *Norwich Mercury* in January 1752, in which Henry Ellison of Norwich, gardener and land surveyor, reported that 'notwithstanding many Reports unfairly spread to the contrary' he undertook:

> *All Sorts of Gardening Works, Wood-Works, Forest Planting, and Planting in all branches whatsoever, in altering old Gardens, as well as making new ones: And when a Survey is taken, he draws and executes any Draught or Plan which shall be approved, viz. Parterres, Kitchen-Gardens, Fruit and Flower-Gardens, Planting of Grandlines, Avenues, Vista's, Serpentine Walks, Groves, Woods, Labyrinths, Porticoe's, Arbours, Salons, Cabinets, Amphitheatios, Platoons, Wildernesses,; and upon proper Situation Water-Works: viz. Aqueducts, Grotto's, Cascades, Canals, Fountains, Basons, Serpentine Rivers and Reservoirs, or any sort of Works that adorn and beautify magnificent Gardens; all which he compleatly finishes after the most modern Taste, and reasonable Prices.*

We must be careful not to exaggerate the extent to which serpentine and irregular forms were adopted, nor the extent to which gardens became less enclosed by walls or hedges in this period. The gardens of the local gentry generally consisted of a number of interlocking enclosures, often with formal planting, well into the 1760s and often beyond.

It was only in the decades after c 1760 that geometric forms and enclosed gardens generally lost their appeal. Gradually, between c 1760 and 1790, most Norfolk landowners of any consequence came to lay out landscape parks around their homes. Yet not only when they did so, but also how, varied considerably from estate to estate. The largest landowners – who, with few exceptions, embraced the new style soon after 1760 – achieved the fashionable setting by softening the geometric structure of planting, removing avenues and any residual walled courts so that the parkland could appear to flow up to

Figure 28
Holkham, Norfolk: William Kent's design for the south garden at Holkham Hall c 1736 (by kind permission of Viscount Coke).

the walls of the house. In such cases, it was pre-existing parkland which, through this process of subtraction, became the sole setting for the mansion (although much new planting, especially of perimeter belts, was usually undertaken). Members of the county elite had all possessed deer parks by the start of the 18th century, some of relatively recent creation, some of medieval origin. The landscape parks of the local gentry, in contrast, were more likely to develop from scratch, at the expense of farmland: comparatively few members of this social group had possessed a deer park.

Systematic surveys of this kind serve to question some of the lines of stylistic descent presented in 18th-century accounts of garden design. Garden historians have often, following Walpole, emphasised the stylistic debt owed by Capability Brown to William Kent, seeing the landscape parks of the former as essentially a development of the small-scale, serpentine, Italianate gardens of the latter. While there is doubtless much truth in this assertion, the real continuity – the real thread – is in the development of the park from the venison farms and hunting grounds of the Middle Ages – to some extent already enjoyed and treated aesthetically – to the deer parks more obviously manipulated aesthetically and which formed the indispensable adjunct to the great mansions of the 17th century. What emerged was the park as the sole, or prime setting for the 18th-century country house. In Norfolk generally, only the landscape parks of the greatest landowners developed di-

rectly from earlier deer parks. Those of the local gentry, however, clearly aped to some extent the appearance of these traditional, and deeply symbolic, landscapes, but without the expensive encumbrance of deer.

Systematic survey reveals other problems with conventional discussions of later 18th-century landscape design. Because garden historians have been so interested in the rise of the landscape park in this period, the development of gardens has often been neglected and occasionally misunderstood. In spite of what is sometimes implied, even at the most fashionable sites, structured gardens did not disappear. They continued to exist, although they were now more serpentine in form and generally located away from the principal façades of the house. François de la Rochefoucauld, visiting Norfolk and Suffolk in 1784, described them:

> *Near the house, usually immediately round it, is what the English call the garden. It is a small pleasure ground, extremely well tended, with little well-rolled gravel paths; the grass is cut every week and the trees, which are of rare kinds, grow there naturally, though every care is taken to prevent moss and ivy growing upon them. In a thousand other ways, too, which one does not notice, care is taken to make these gardens attractive. Flowers are planted in them ...(Scarfe 1988, 34–5).*

At some less 'fashionable' sites, older walled gardens might be retained, even though a land-

49

scape park had been laid out. Where this occurred, the parkland generally extended away to the south of the house, with fragments of the older network of walled enclosures being retained to the north, or to the sides – as at Intwood, Hedenham, or Kirby Cane. With such an arrangement the owners could have their cake and eat it: they could enjoy the fashionable public prospect over open parkland while still savouring the delights of structured gardens in more private locations (Williamson 1995, 87–92).

In addition, it is clear that the kitchen garden gained, or maintained, an aesthetic and recreational role as the other yards and enclosures around the house were removed. Kitchen gardens were normally a feature of the circuit walks leading through, and out of, the pleasure grounds near the house. In 1789, Repton advised against extending the proposed walks around the lake at Holkham as far as the kitchen garden on Howe Hill; but only until the farm buildings next to it had been removed, something which was in fact done soon afterwards (Red Book, Holkham Hall Library). Five years later, in April 1794, William Windham visited Holkham and 'walked before dinner into the kitchen garden' (just as, four years later, he recorded how he went out riding at Felbrigg and returned via the greenhouse 'to gather a nosegay') (Baring 1866, 121). For it was not just vegetables that were grown within the box-edged beds, but also flowers of various kinds. At Felbrigg, for example, a description of the kitchen gardens made in 1781 noted that 'down the middle and cross walks on both sides are borders of flowers' (NRO WKC7/156/3, 404 X 8). Contrary to what is sometimes suggested, walled kitchen gardens were rarely banished to some distant recess of the park. They usually remained close to the mansion, albeit tucked away behind a screen of shrubbery or plantation (or the stable block). Less than 10% of 18th-century country houses studied in this survey had kitchen gardens which could seriously be described as 'detached', in the sense that they lay more than 250 m from the mansion house.

The role of kitchen gardens as places for display as well as production explains, in part, the phenomenal sums spent on their construction. That built in the 1780s at Holkham, designed by the prestigious architect Samuel Wyatt, reputedly cost no less than £10,000 to build and equip (Wade Martins 1983, 22). Even on small estates, the sums were often large. At Heacham, the kitchen garden cost over £898 in the 1770s (NRO HEA 489) – nearly as much as the entire park – while that at Salle, although covering little more than an acre, cost its owner, William Hase, £565 in the 1760s (NRO MC 65/1).

Systematic surveys not only allow us to chart, with some confidence, the way that the grounds of landowners changed in the course of the 18th

century, they also encourage us to place these designs in their wider social, economic and landscape contexts. The distribution of designed landscapes is a particularly interesting, but rather neglected, topic. In terms of the density and distribution of landscape parks, Norfolk can be divided into three kinds of region (Fig 29). Firstly, there were those districts in which, by the end of the 18th century, there were few parks of any kind, and those which did exist were small. The Fenlands in the far west of the county, the area of Flegg and the Norfolk Broads to the east, and the level clay plateau in the centre-south, all fall into this category. Secondly, there were those areas – on the more dissected clay soils, especially to the south west of Norwich, and on the sandy heaths to the north of the city – in which there were large numbers of parks of all sizes. The density of parks in these areas was, in general, around one for every 25 km². Lastly, there were those areas – the 'Good Sands' in the north west of the county, and Breckland immediately to the south of this – in which there were moderate numbers of parks, but a high proportion in the highest size category.

This pattern seems to be the consequence of a number of factors. By and large, regions in which there were few parks, and none in the highest size category, were those in which the post-medieval economy had been geared to cattle husbandry – a form of agriculture which, all things being equal, tended in the 16th and 17th centuries to encourage the survival of smaller estates and freehold farmers (Allison 1957; Holderness 1984; Thirsk 1970). In arable areas, in contrast – especially those with relatively poor soils – large estates came, in the course of the post-medieval period, to dominate the landscape. Such regional variations in farming were breaking down in the second half of the 18th century when East Anglia, as a whole, became an increasingly arable region. Earlier structures of ownership were only slowly modified, in part because other factors worked to discourage the development of large estates in formerly pastoral areas. The Fens, the Flegg/Broadland area of east Norfolk and the southern clays were all districts in which soils were comparatively fertile, and land prices relatively high. They had, even in the Middle Ages, been the least manorialised areas of the county (Williamson 1993, 163–80). Long-term features of tenurial organisation, medium-term trends in agrarian specialisation, and the direct impact of land values together ensured that these were districts in which large or medium-sized landed estates, and therefore landscape parks, remained rare.

But the distribution of 18th-century parks can only be partly explained in terms of soil-types and agrarian regions. Because many landowners possessed properties in more than one part of the county, the distribution of parks was, to some

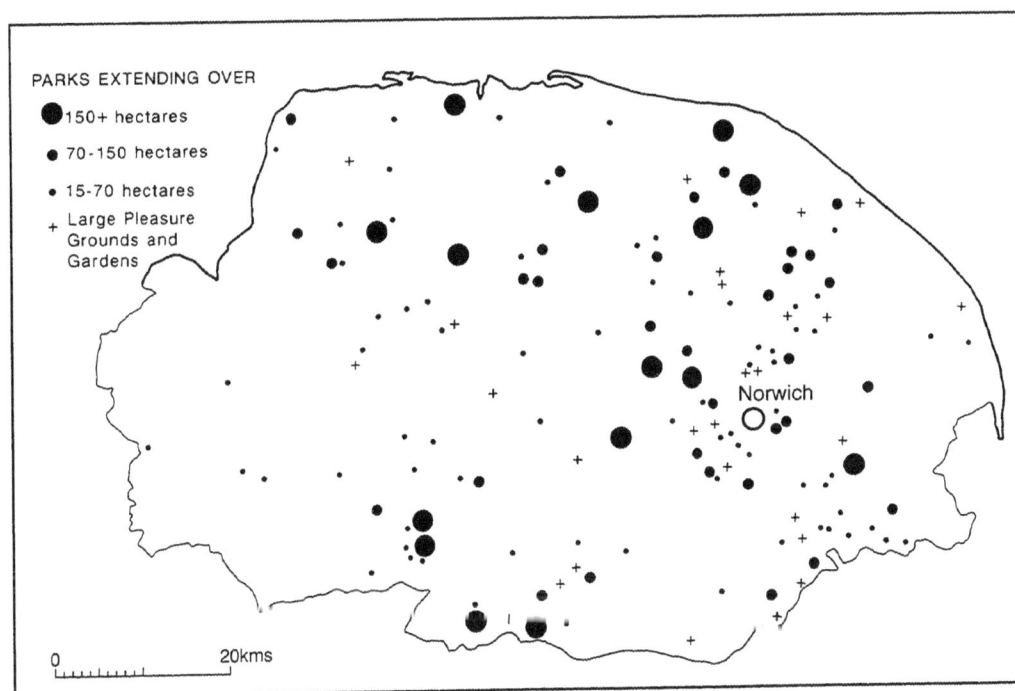

Figure 29
The distribution of landscape parks in Norfolk, c 1795, as depicted on William Faden's county map.

extent, a function of residential choice. On the one hand, it is noticeable that the least undulating parts of the county – Fenland, the Broads, the Southern Plateau – were those in which there were fewest parks; on the other, it is striking how parks were densely clustered in the vicinity of Norwich. Just under a third of the parks in the county were located within 15 km of the city, a comfortable ride away; 43% lay within 20 km. This is an unsurprising observation, perhaps, in this age of fashionable consumerism and of the increasing commercialisation of leisure.

Multi-disciplinary regional surveys have a number of other advantages. They encourage us to interpret designed landscapes not only in terms of elite aesthetic theory, but also in terms of local social history. When we examine diaries, forestry records, farming accounts and memoranda books we soon learn the extent to which the features around the homes of the aristocracy and gentry were not simply disposed in order to create a pleasing prospect. These objects and spaces were also used, both economically and recreationally: such activities could have an important and, at times, determining influence on their layout. Thus, to take one example, there is little doubt that the disposition of clumps and belts within and around Norfolk's landscape parks was partly determined by the needs of shooting, a pastime which had, by the end of the 18th century, become an obsession among local landowners.

THE ARCHAEOLOGICAL CONTRIBUTION

A regional study broadens our perspective, changes our agenda, and shows us *general* patterns which can help us to interpret the *particular*

examples of designed landscapes. What can archaeology – using the term in its widest sense, to include the study of all surviving physical features, including planting – contribute to such a project?

Firstly, archaeological survey can supply information about gardens for which we have no other record, especially those predating the early to mid 18th century. Such gardens often featured terraces, basins, paths and other hard landscaping, particularly accessible to conventional archaeological enquiry. In Norfolk, as elsewhere, such features survive best where owners lacked the resources to obliterate earlier remains effectively, when fashions changed in the later 18th century. Even on well-documented sites, archaeology can fill in gaps in the written and pictorial record: in particular, archaeological evidence can often help to differentiate between those archive maps which are 'real' estate surveys, and those which are unexecuted proposals. Even where there are contemporary maps or illustrations of lost gardens, archaeology can provide a more accurate representation of a design. At Rougham, for example, a faded estate map of 1734 (private collection) is too schematic to allow us to see the complex, abstract geometry underlying the plan of the gardens, designed around 1700, by architect and writer, Roger North (Williamson 1996).

More importantly, archaeology is often our best, sometimes our only, source of information about the pre-park landscape: the working countryside which existed before a park was laid out. Parks can act, as others in this volume have emphasised, as the 'guardians of early landscapes', and this is particularly true in an intensively arable county like Norfolk, where parks today often constitute the *only* area of permanent

51

grass of any size in a parish. The largest surviving areas of ridge and furrow in the county are thus all to be found in parks. Such relict landscapes (Fig 30) are interesting in their own right, but they are also of vital significance in understanding the development of the designed landscapes, for these are the remains of the place whose 'genius' was consulted by owners and designers. Over and over again we can see how the form of a landscape park was influenced by the layout of features in the earlier countryside. At Holkham, for example, the great belt planted in the 1790s linked a number of areas of pre-existing woodland. Similarly, at Great Melton, the clumps in the north park were positioned, not according to the discerning eye of the artist, nor in imitation of some Lorraine painting, but so as to obscure a scatter of earlier marl pits. Above all, in park after park, the earliest maps reveal that the majority of the timber stood, and often still stands, in straight lines: field survey reveals the survivors, ancient pollards, standing on the flattened remains of hedge banks. Why plant new trees, when old ones were already to hand?

Among the earthworks of the earlier landscape encountered in Norfolk parks are a number of deserted settlements. Indeed, between a quarter and a third of the deserted, or severely shrunken, villages known in the county probably lie within areas which were, by the late 18th century, occupied by landscape parks. Yet we must be very careful about how we interpret this evidence, for in only six or seven cases can it be shown that desertion was *caused* by emparking.

The relationship is in fact a highly complex one: parks and settlement desertion or shrinkage tend to occur in the same areas, but the creation of the former did not necessarily cause the latter. Rather, both were often quite separate manifestations of strong, undivided ownership. Shrunken villages tended to have single owners in the post-medieval period: and single owners tended to limit or further reduce the size of villages, partly to restrict the number of potential claimants of poor relief and thus the magnitude of the Poor Rate (Holderness 1972). The removal of individual farms and cottages to make way for parks was relatively common. However, the obliteration or relocation of entire settlements was comparatively rare in Norfolk, in part perhaps because the dispersed character of the local settlement pattern (and the isolated position of many manor houses) made it unnecessary.

Even where villages were removed for emparking, as at Houghton (Fig 31), they had usually experienced prior shrinkage for the kinds of reasons just mentioned (a pattern paralleled elsewhere: Taylor 1983a, 211). Interestingly, the long-abandoned portion of the village here survives as prominent earthworks: the area around the parish church, cleared in the 1720s for the expansion of the park, was deliberately levelled – a fate shared by most other villages in the county cleared for emparking in the early or middle decades of the 18th century. At Holkham, for example, there is now no above-ground trace of Holkham village in the vicinity of the hall. The labourers worked long and hard to eradicate all

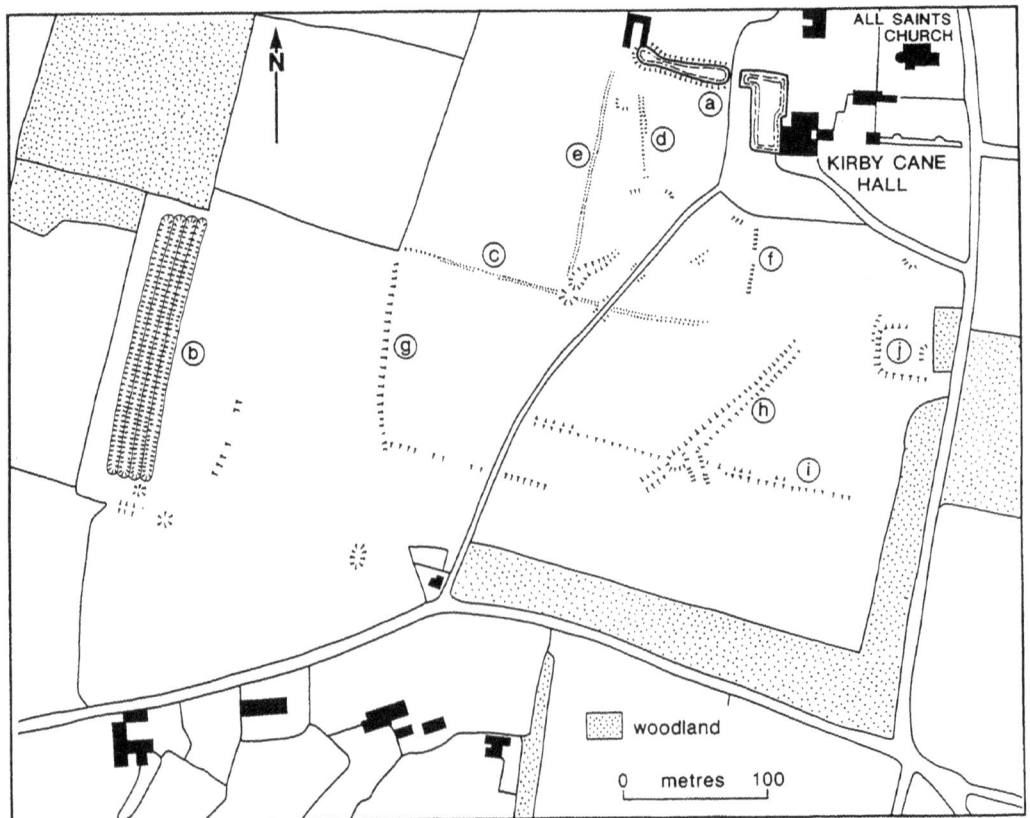

Figure 30
Kirby Cane, Norfolk: relict landscape features, preserved as earthworks within the park: (a) remains of a moat; (b) ridge and furrow; (c)-(g), (i) relict field boundaries; (h) former roadway; (j) possible farm site.

52

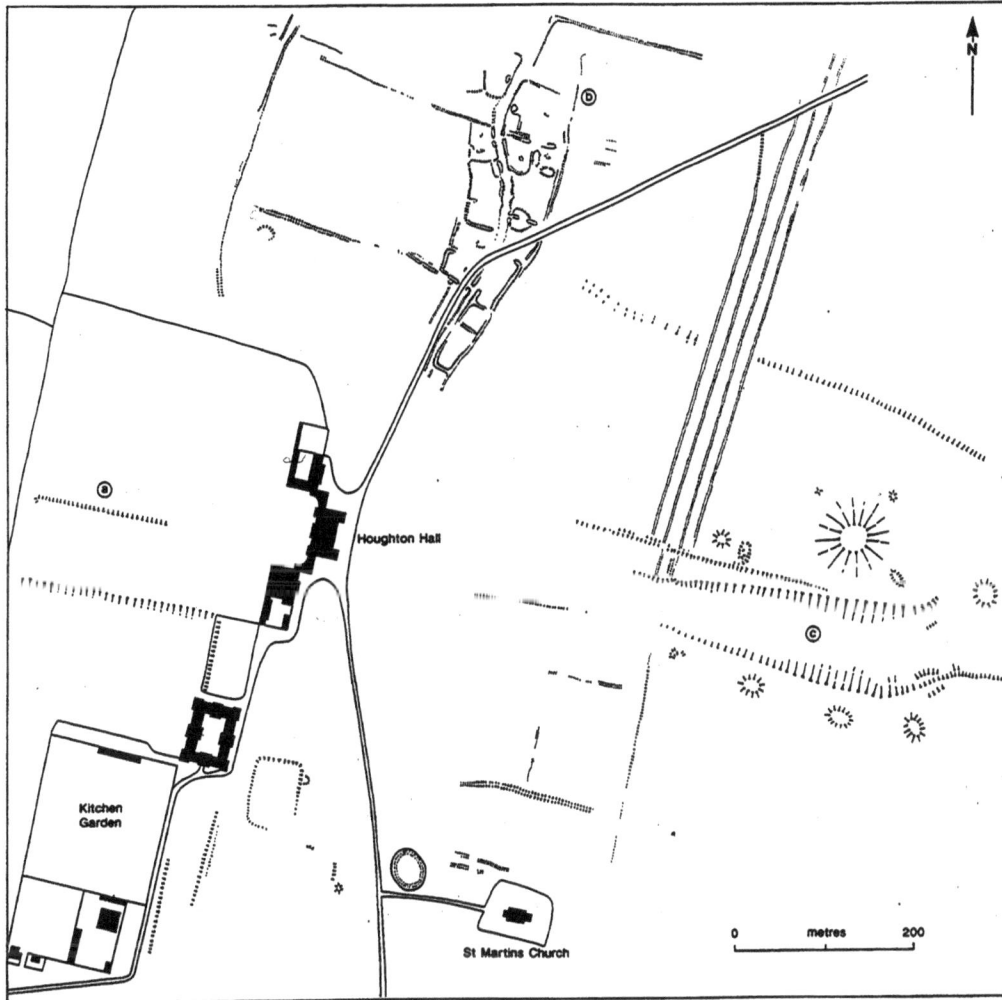

Figure 31
Houghton Park, Norfolk: principal earthwork features: (a) early 18th-century garden terraces; (b) area of settlement desertion; (c) cutting made in the 1740s to improve the east prospect from the hall. Other earthworks include relict field boundaries and earlier park boundaries. Only slight traces survive of the village removed in the 1720s from the vicinity of St Martin's church.

signs of their own homes after these had been cleared away in the 1720s. In archaeological terms, the interesting thing here is the *absence of evidence*.

Archaeological analysis can also be of immense importance in understanding the development of walled gardens, amplifying the evidence already briefly outlined for the continuing popularity of such features during the second half of the 18th century. At Intwood, for example, what has been described as a '17th-century walled garden' is, in fact, a complex, multi-period structure, maintained, repaired, and even added to, in the later 18th century (Fig 32). Kitchen gardens of 18th-century date can also repay close scrutiny. That at Heydon, probably constructed shortly before 1776, has a small conservatory built into, and apparently contemporary with, its north wall: a building clearly intended for the enjoyment of ornamental plants. Even a cursory examination of these structures reveals the considerable care and attention devoted to their layout and design in this period, clearly reflecting their importance as part of the landscape of fashion. While many kitchen gardens were of simple rectangular form, a significant number displayed different, sometimes eccentric layouts. Some adopted a trapezoid form: that built at

Raynham in the 1780s was so trapezoidal in shape that it appears in plan almost as a truncated triangle. Another group of variants has one or more curved walls; examples include those at High House West Acre, Barningham, and Raveningham. At Wood Hall, Hilgay, the gardens are almost oval in plan. These variations all appear to have been intended to increase the length of south-facing walls. Interestingly, they do not seem to have been based on plans in published texts (which generally recommended a rectangular plan, ranged east–west on a south-facing slope). Rather, they indicate a measure of enthusiastic inventiveness on the part of owners and gardeners, reflecting a continuing engagement with the walled garden, hidden though it might now be from sight of the open parkland.

THEORY AND PRACTICE

So far I have discussed matters of archaeological practice: the recording and surveying of physical traces of past human activity. But archaeological *theory* is also important in understanding these remains. We need to think about these landscapes in the kinds of ways that prehistorians, like John Barrett, approach the great monuments of neolithic Wessex (Barrett 1994). How were they

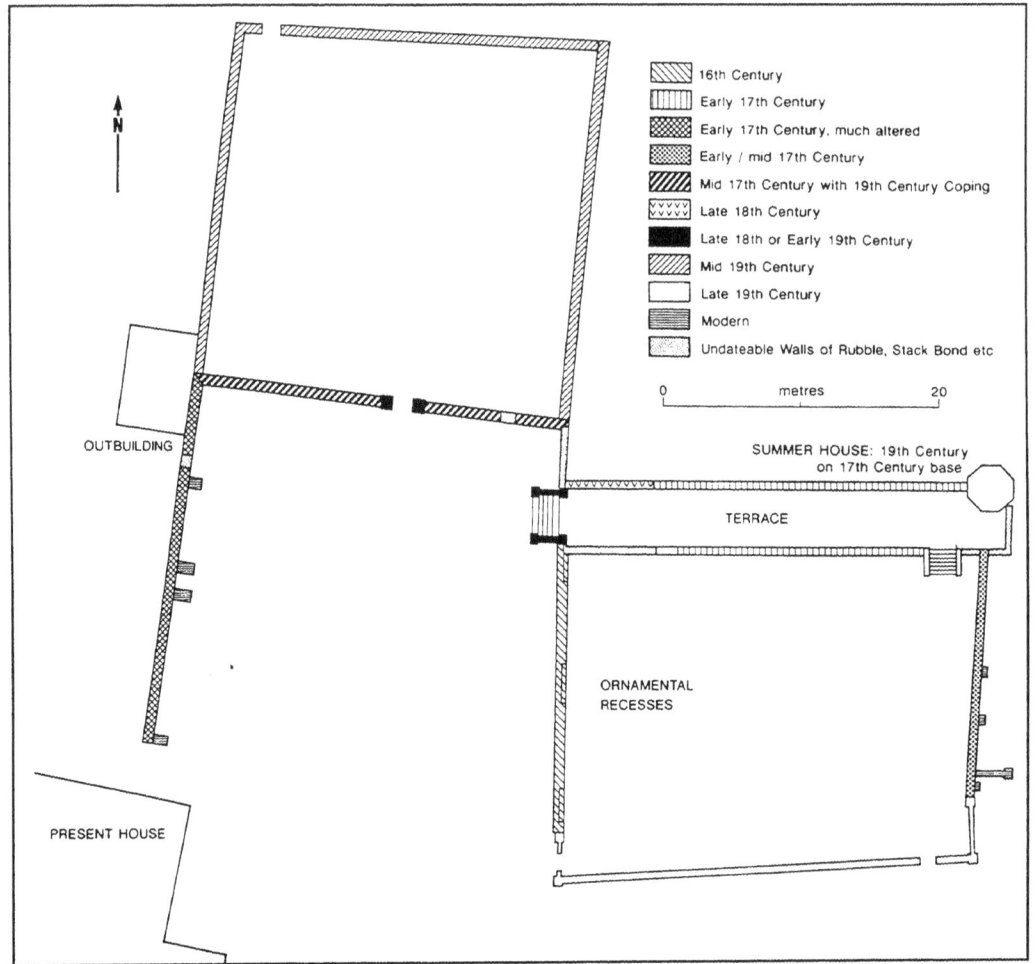

16th Century
Early 17th Century
Early 17th Century, much altered
Early / mid 17th Century
Mid 17th Century with 19th Century Coping
Late 18th Century
Late 18th or Early 19th Century
Mid 19th Century
Late 19th Century
Modern
Undateable Walls of Rubble, Stack Bond etc

0   metres   20

SUMMER HOUSE: 19th Century
on 17th Century base

OUTBUILDING

TERRACE

ORNAMENTAL
RECESSES

PRESENT HOUSE

Figure 32
Intwood, Norfolk:
the walled garden.

perceived and experienced by the various social actors moving within, or excluded from them? What messages were they supposed to convey: about their owners, about their owners' relationships with neighbours and with the world at large? And to whom were such messages directed? When William Kent laid out the elaborate serpentine garden to the south of Holkham Hall in the late 1730s and early 40s (Fig 28), he was creating an idealised image of the Italian landscape, a three-dimensional version of a painting by Poussin or Lorraine. The resulting ensemble would have meant one thing to visiting members of the elite who had been on the Grand Tour – it constituted, in effect, a romanticised image of a half-remembered visit, a kind of blurred three-dimensional postcard. It meant something else to other visitors to this theatre of landscape – the local gentry and the urban patriciate of King's Lynn or Norwich – whose familiarity with such scenes was vicarious and enjoyed through the medium of prints based on fashionable paintings. To them, the act of recognition would both have affirmed Coke's membership of a wealthy and travelled elite, together with their own relatively knowledgeable and comparatively elevated position. The garden would have meant something else again to the local community, particularly to the labourers who constructed it, and in

so doing eradicated the physical traces of their own history. Such landscapes were taken out of history – taken out of real time and made unknowable to all but the educated. At Houghton, even the medieval church, marooned within the park, was largely rebuilt – to designs by Thomas Ripley – so that it might better conform to some abstract elite concept of medieviality (Yaxley 1994). We can take these landscapes too much for granted: we should try to recapture the shock that they must have made when new. They are now too familiar, too much a part of 'our' heritage, that we sometimes miss their essential strangeness. They were strange in other ways. Holkham Hall and its landscape were begun in 1722 and completed in 1761, yet few visitors complained that the place was a permanent building site. Instead, they enthused over the steadily or rather, unsteadily unrolling display of taste; for the archaeological evidence, in particular, shows that there were innumerable changes in plan, as fashions changed before ambitious projects could be completed. The doing of the project was as important as its completion: these landscapes were about becoming, as much as being.

The landscape parks which proliferated in Norfolk during the second half of the 18th century are simpler landscapes, but they also have a story to tell. They reflect their owners' attitudes to the earlier landscape, to the surrounding landscape, to social equals and superiors, and to the poor. The message conveyed by surrounding a mansion with a cordon of grass and trees was plain enough: by secluding their homes from those of the local community, and from the fields of their labour, landowners affirmed their membership of a particular social group – the broad, late 18th-century elite of the 'polite'. But here again the wider landscape context is important. Although generally ignored by garden historians, the destruction of walled gardens at these sites was almost invariably accompanied by the thoroughgoing removal of all useful signs of industry from the vicinity of the house – namely barns, yards, dovecotes, fishponds and orchards. The gentry thus placed themselves within landscapes which – ostensibly at least – shunned all involvement in the humdrum practicalities of agrarian life. Similarly, at a time when gardens were increasing in elaboration and sophistication among the middle class – and social complexity and mobility were increasing – the removal of structured gardens from the main façades made important statements about the distinctive nature of landownership (Williamson 1995, 109–18). These are all matters which concern the relationship between society and material culture: they are thus archaeological questions. If we seek only to record and catalogue traces of past activity, we are not doing our full job. The landscape is the archaeology: the earthworks are only a part of it, albeit a vital one.

Theory is one thing. Making archaeology of some practical use in the present is another. Yet the contribution made by survey and research to the conservation and restoration of designed landscapes is not always entirely straightforward. Most of the sites examined in the course of this survey were complex, multi-period palimpsests. This perception of complexity is only increased by detailed investigation, serving to raise, in particularly acute form, the question of what period we should restore a particular landscape to. Should we simply fossilise it in the form it is now, categorising it as an historical landscape whose development, almost by definition, is over? Or should we remove modern accretions and return it to some arbitrary point in the relatively recent past: as it was when surveyed for the OS first edition 6-inch map in the 19th century, for example? Neither approach is exactly easy to justify in philosophical terms, and when sites remain in private ownership there are practical difficulties

too. Owners, understandably, want to leave their own mark on a landscape created by previous generations of their family. They want to make their own contribution to the developing palimpsest. They want to plant *leylandii* hedges, and avenues of flowering cherries. Detailed archaeological and documentary research can help little: by producing yet more evidence for a long and complex history of change, the argument against fossilisation seems strengthened. When presented with such evidence, one estate manager recently responded: 'good: we can go on making changes'.

We should also be aware that archaeology – using this term in the widest sense – never gives the full picture and can present a misleading one. The planting which survives from the 18th century, in the smaller Norfolk parks, is overwhelmingly dominated by oaks, a large proportion of which are ancient pre-park pollards. Some beech and sweet chestnut also remain, especially in the perimeter belts, together with sporadic examples of London plane, lime and cedar of Lebanon. But where are all the Scots pines, silver fir, larch, Lombardy poplars, and other horrors which were also – to judge from the documentary evidence – freely planted in the open parkland? The short-lived nature of much 18th-century planting poses particular problems for restoration. William Kent's clumps on the North Lawn at Holkham consisted of magnificent stands of beech when they were described and photographed in the later 19th century. We can plot the position of lost trees from the remains of their stumps and their restoration is currently underway. Yet Kent's original drawing, and the details provided by the estate accounts, leave little doubt that the beech clumps were originally envisaged as more complex features, also containing silver fir, larch, and Scots pine – all relatively short-lived species, chosen to provide an instant effect. The 'restoration' of such features is highly problematic. The re-establishment of beech is the obvious and easiest solution; but should we, in fact, replant as Kent intended, in the full knowledge that we will need to replant again within a generation or so?

I don't know the answers: these are deep and difficult questions. What I can say, from the East Anglian experience, is that archaeology has a vital role to play in understanding the history of parks and gardens. The contribution it can make to practical matters, of curation and restoration, can at times be more problematic: for as with all things, the more we know, the less easy decisions become.

TWO RELICT GARDENS IN SOMERSET: THEIR CHANGING FORTUNES THROUGH THE 17TH AND 18TH CENTURIES AS REVEALED BY FIELD EVIDENCE AND OTHER SOURCES
Robert Wilson-North

ABSTRACT

Recent fieldwork in Somerset shows how earthwork survey plays a vital co-ordinating role in the non-invasive investigation of relict gardens and in the coherent application of sometimes apparently disparate sources. The resulting interpretation of complex sites allows an important body of information to be brought to the attention of both garden and architectural historians as well as archaeologists.

INTRODUCTION

Fieldwork by the RCHME during the 1970s led to the unavoidable realisation that the earthwork remains of relict gardens are a recurring aspect of the English landscape. Since that pioneering fieldwork by Chris Taylor and others, independent excavation and other archaeological research has taken place, so that the study of abandoned gardens can now truly be said to be part of the discipline of archaeology.

However, the archaeological study of gardens has shifted towards detailed excavation and restoration projects at a very few sites, whilst much still remains to be done in the detailed non-invasive recording of completely abandoned gardens. The present trend of research and archaeological activity has been away from fieldwork and a greater balance needs to be achieved. It is certainly time to reassert the contribution which non-invasive fieldwork can make and it is appropriate to stress this in the papers of a conference which has so successfully brought field archaeologists and garden historians together.

This paper shows the enormous potential contained in the earthworks of relict gardens and the importance of analytical fieldwork in their understanding. The examples used have been surveyed by the RCHME's Exeter Office and they have been chosen to support and illustrate the themes of this paper. However, it is worth stressing that the fieldwork was carried out for other reasons: one as part of an internal project on Carthusian monasteries, the other as a request from Somerset County Council.

Both sites discussed here have substantial 17th or 18th-century phases, but are more typically characterised by the complexity of the sequence they represent. This very complexity has often lead to erroneous interpretation or even the inability to understand what is there, a factor which has thus far denied such sites from the studies of garden historians.

The starting point for the study of abandoned gardens, at least for the RCHME, is usually the requirement to make a record of what survives in the landscape. Field survey, therefore, plays a central part in the process of investigation. In later periods in particular, an accurate plan of the earthworks is vital to the interpretation of other forms of evidence – whether it be the results of other modern surveys, such as geophysical survey or arboricultural surveys, or whether it be in the precise application of historical sources, such as contemporary maps, plans, views or descriptions. Indeed, in all the cases discussed, the quality of the results relies heavily on the combination of various sources of evidence and methodologies; but in each, a metrically accurate plan of the earthworks enables such an integrated approach to achieve its full potential.

WITHAM, SOMERSET

At Witham, near Frome (NGR ST 758 417), an earthwork survey was carried out on the site of England's first Carthusian monastery, as part of a national project by the RCHME and Bristol University to record the remains of this religious order in England.

Previous work on the site had been directed solely at the identification of the monastic remains. This had taken the form of excavations, in the 1920s and 1960s, on the north side of the Great Cloister, where parts of what were assumed to be the principal conventual buildings were discovered (Burrow and Burrow 1990). The excavators' interpretation fitted their expectations of the archaeology and those of the era in which they worked: little attempt was made to record the later, post-monastic phases.

More recently, the fashion for garden archaeology led to the recognition that a post-Dissolution sequence existed at Witham, but no detailed analysis of it had been attempted (Bond and Iles 1991, 50).

The RCHME survey confirmed that some of the earthworks, which lie within a precisely rectangular field, are indeed the remains of elaborate gardens and walks. This layout was understood by establishing the whereabouts of the house that once stood there, a house known to architectural historians through a fine elevation drawing and plan of 1717, carried out for the owner, William Wyndham, by the architect James Gibbs (Figs 33 and 34). During fieldwork,

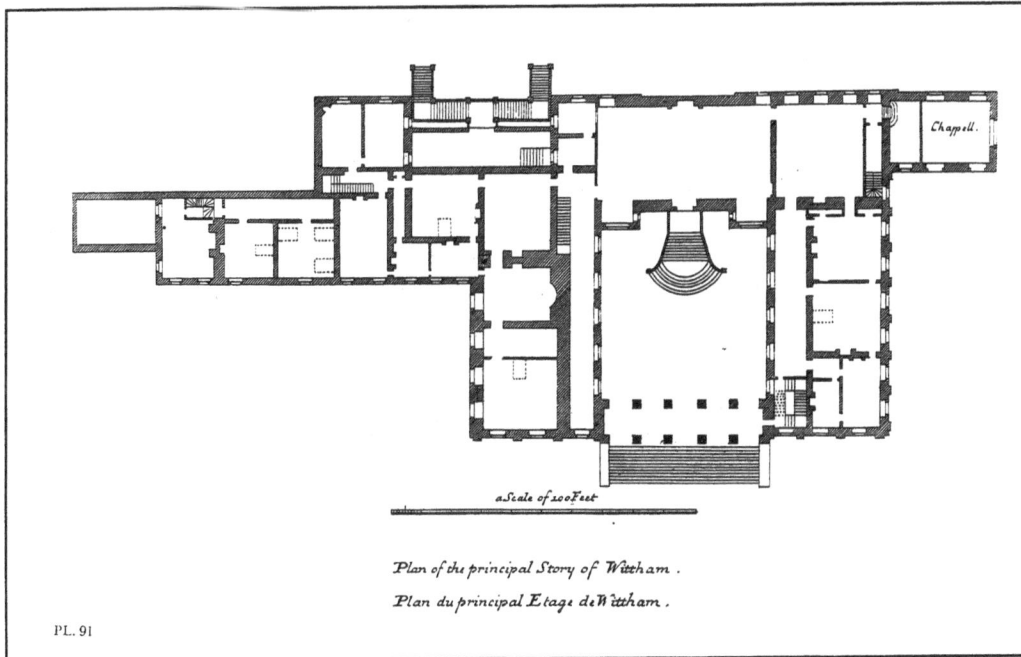

Figure 33
Witham, Somerest: James Gibbs' plan of the house (Campbell 1725, II, pl.91) .

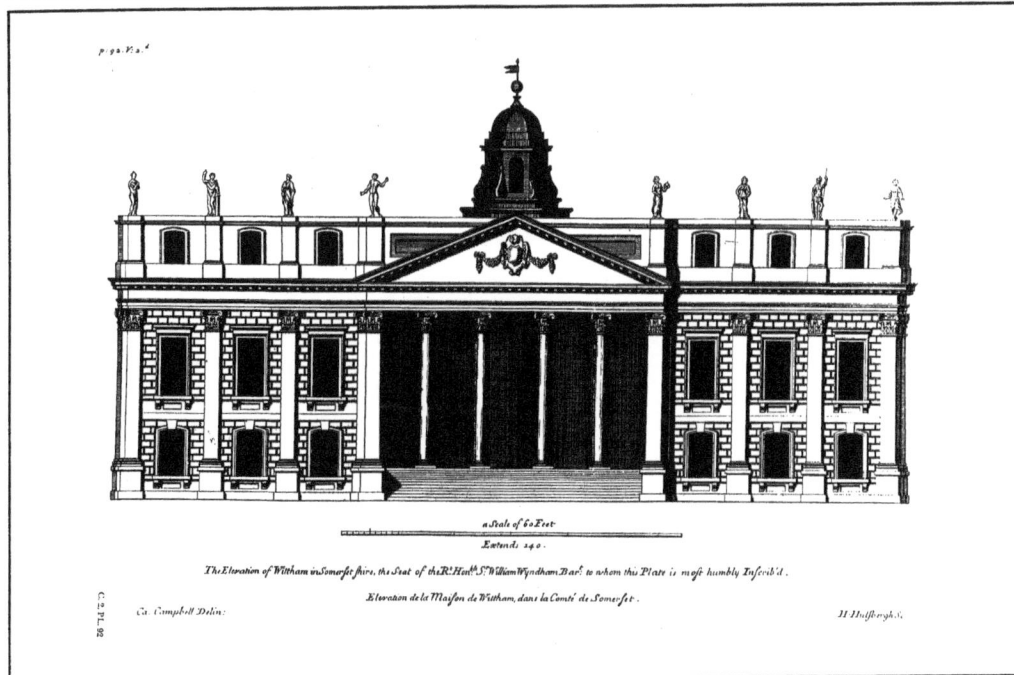

Figure 34
Witham, Somerset: James Gibbs' elevation drawing of the house (Campbell 1725, II, pl. 92).

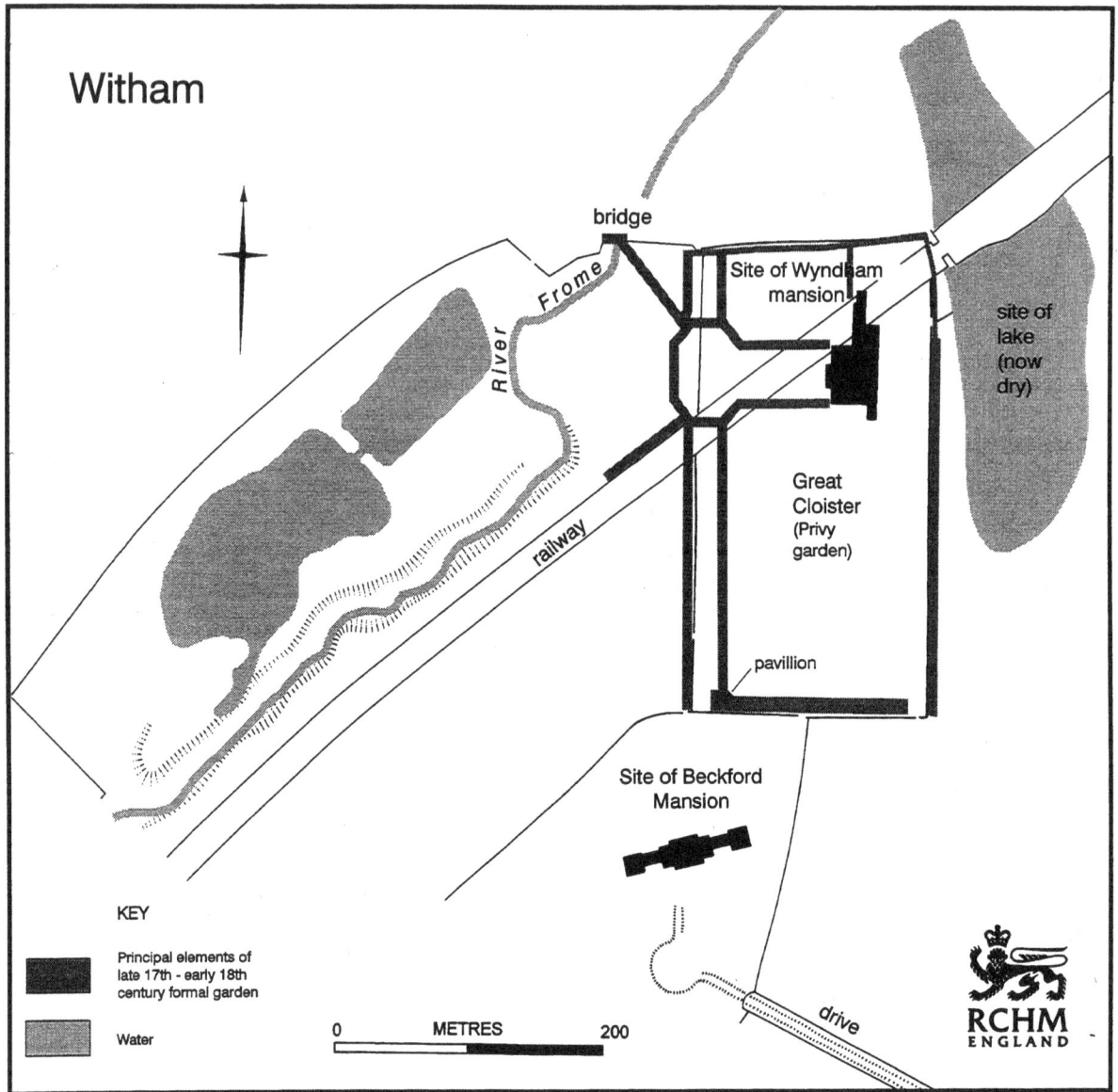

Witham

KEY

Principal elements of
late 17th - early 18th
century formal garden

Water

0   METRES   200

RCHM
ENGLAND

Figure 35
Witham, Somerset:
simplified interpretation
plan, showing houses,
garden and lakes
(RCHME, © Crown
copyright).

its precise position was established as an area of earthworks, on the northern side of the Great Cloister. Subsequent geophysical survey revealed buried walls (Gaffney 1994), which not only confirmed the existence of the house, but also that it was built to the plan of 1717.

The survey also showed that a rectangular area to the west, bisected diagonally by the railway line, was the entrance court. Not only had the whereabouts of the house been established, on the site of the Carthusian priory but so, too, had its orientation, which allowed a closer analysis of how the house interplayed with the gardens (Wilson-North 1996).

The house was the focal point of the garden layout, standing on a spur flanked to west and east by substantial sheets of water (Fig 35). To the west of the house lay the outer court. This survives as a flat rectangular compartment 58 m by 40 m, the western end of which was probably embellished with an octagonal area. From here, the principal drive, surviving as a raised bank, led

north-westwards to a bridge over the River Frome. It seems that the intention was to create a series of lakes within the valley of the Frome, but the meandering river was initially an obstruction to this plan. The problem was solved by moving the river to one side of the valley and diverting it into a massive cutting, thereby allowing the construction of a pair of lakes which could be seen from the house and its main approach. Significantly, the eastern end of the lowest lake has been skewed to make it more visible when viewed from that direction, and so enhance the vista. At this point the river has a pronounced meander, emphasising the prospect from the house. The lakes were clearly intended to be perambulated: the dams form terraces and access to them was probably via a stone bridge across the river, at their eastern end. A second terrace, described in 1812 as the 'Terras Field' (SRO DD/X/MGR no 1: Map of Witham Estate by Francis Webb), lay on the southern side of the lakes and was later obliterated by the railway line.

Thus, the porticoed 'Front to the gardens', mentioned in the 18th century by Colen Campbell (1771), looked across the entrance court and octagon, to the pair of lakes beyond and along the valley of the Frome, towards the distant prospect of Witham Friary church. It not only provided the main entrance to the house, but also overlooked a principal aspect of the ornamental setting. The discovery of this hitherto unknown main vista was made possible through the process of locating the house, a factor which itself probably suggests a contemporary date for the gardens – at the beginning of the 18th century.

The gardens seen from the west front were, however, only a part of the layout. To the east, a series of ponds in the valley of a tributary of the River Frome, and the area of the present rectangular field, were further important elements. This rectangular field probably perpetuates the extent of the Carthusian precinct. Its edges are defined by broad, terraced walks and at the highest point, in the south-western corner, a square mound is the site of a pavilion or summer house, which overlooked the formal gardens, lakes and house. The Great Cloister continued as a privy garden, adjacent to the south wing of the house. It was reached from the east of the house by a terrace that continued along the east side of the garden, looking down on the southernmost of the ponds. The geophysical survey revealed traces of a symmetrical layout of beds and paths within the cloister. They form a principal north–south path bisecting the rectangle, with a number of other features running east–west at right angles to it. There are traces of diagonal features at the corners.

The 1960s exacavations uncovered a monastic pavement *in situ* in the Great Cloister garth, with a coin of 1672 upon it. This strengthens the impression that the former cloister walk served as a garden walk and there is further intriguing evidence from a 1760s survey, which includes a valuation of lead on the premises (SRO DD/WYp, Box 1, p15 pt 3: Survey and Valuation of Witham Hall by Thomas Browne 1762). It lists almost two tons of lead 'on the ridge and on the Cornish over the Terras Walk', indicating that some of the walk was roofed and raising the possibility that part of the covered cloister walk survived for more than 200 years after the Dissolution.

Thus, from the combined evidence of earthwork and geophysical survey, contemporary engravings and excavated evidence, a tentative picture of the magnificent gardens at Witham Hall begins to emerge. The importance of the 1717 plan cannot be overstressed: it is central to the process of understanding Witham, but had been put aside by earlier researchers, simply because the whereabouts of the house was not known. Earthwork and geophysical survey established where the house was and, crucially, that it had been built as the plan indicated. With its

validity confirmed, it could no longer be seen simply as a design of what Wyndham intended, but a source of information about what was there, containing clues about the development of the building. The plan distinguishes wall thicknesses, and a substantial compartment in its northern wing is massively constructed, confirming a contemporary account of the 'Old Dark Vaulted Carthusian chapell' on the north side of the quadrangle (Strachey undated). Once the survey had located and orientated the house, this contemporary account made sense, and the Carthusian church could be identified for the first time, contradicting the conclusions of the 1960s excavations. This discovery had been made through rigorous application of good quality source material, combined with thorough non-invasive field techniques. But its implications went further than the Carthusian monastery or the house built for William Wyndham.

Sir William Wyndham's elder son, Charles, who succeeded his uncle as Earl of Egremont, sold the property in 1761 to William Beckford, a merchant who was Lord Mayor of London in 1762 and 1769. He resolved to erect a mansion on a new site at Witham and commissioned Robert Adam to design it.

The house was to be built on the summit of a gently rounded hill, giving it a prominent aspect and one that exploited the local topography to achieve a balanced sense of landscape. This was in contrast to the earlier house, which occupied a more introverted setting within the valley of the Frome – a private and secluded place that followed from its origins as a Carthusian priory.

The new house consisted of a central block with flanking pavilions (Fig 35), a typically Palladian layout and one frequently used by Adam in his designs for country houses. Despite assumptions that the Adam house was not built (Spiers 1979, 31), its site was in fact known before the RCHME survey. It is marked by a pronounced mound containing a massive trench, in a field south of the Wyndhams' house. Unfortunately, the area was infilled by Frome District Council in the 1960s and the earthworks are now obscured. Fortunately, however, air photographs from the 1940s show it more clearly and a transcription of this information (Winton 1994) reveals the unmistakable shape of the house, even down to the location of the perron staircases on the main front. This evidence confirms that the basement storey, at least, was built, but Collinson writes that the principal entrance was flanked by semi-circular columns 'which reared their rich and lofty capitals almost to the top of the edifice'. If the walls were as complete as this comment implies, then the building may have been roofed as a matter of priority, to prevent rapid deterioration.

The intention must have been to create a park for the Adam house. Collinson wrote that the building was 'situated in the upper part of what was intended to be an extensive and beautiful lawn'. Little trace of the park survives in the modern landscape, and it is probable that not a great deal had been done before work on the house was halted. However, a green lane, approaching from Gaer Hill some 2.5 km to the east, perpetuates the former drive. It is straight for 2 km, passing through an area known as Witham Park that was still open ground in 1812 (SRO DD/X/MGR no 1: Map of Witham Estate by Francis Webb), before turning abruptly from this course to climb the hill to the site of the Adam mansion. The straight stretch is aligned precisely on the site of the Wyndham house, presumably the intention being to use some feature there for an eyecatcher within the park, providing a distant prospect beyond the drive.

It may be doubted whether the old house would have provided a suitable focus, even as a ruin. More probably, Adam – or whoever conceived the park – was impressed by the remains of the Carthusian monastery entombed within the house, as described by Strachey, and revealed by the 1717 plan. Adam's intention was to strip away the mouldering post-Dissolution house to reveal the remains of the monastery as a real gothick folly but this was apparently never executed. It is difficult to explain the alignment of the drive in any other way.

A gothick folly, based on the monastic remains, would not have been untypical of Adam. His work for the Earl of Northumberland at Alnwick included a tall stone gothick tower and unexecuted designs for a spectacular castellated eyecatcher on a nearby crag. The only 'ruined' building by Adam of this kind, is the ruined arch and viaduct over a ravine leading to Culzean Castle in Ayrshire.

The landscape at Witham, therefore, contains a range of elements. Its earthworks represent a series of phases of buildings and gardens, all ultimately influenced by the monastic plan, which although no longer existing, could still dictate the position of Robert Adam's great drive some 600 years later. It is the rich complexity of this evidence which makes the physical remains so difficult to disentangle.

The work provides an especially notable example of archaeological field survey, itself deploying and integrating a range of techniques, able to unlock a series of problems and to supply conclusive new interpretations of the evidence.

LOW HAM, SOMERSET

Low Ham, or historically, 'Netherham', is on the floodplain of a tributary of the River Parrett on the edge of the Somerset Levels (NGR ST 433 291). The complicated earthworks represent a sequence of formal gardens, dating from the late 16th century to the end of the 17th century, a sequence that was ultimately left unfinished.

The medieval history of Low Ham is dominated by its owners, the Berkeley family. The estate descended to Henry, Lord Compton, who by 1588 had sold it to Edward Hext; he resided there until his death in 1625 (Aston 1978, 21). The mansion was considered one of the finest houses in the west of England (Collinson 1791, 444–6), but its size, appearance and precise site are not known. Edward Hext was also responsible for refurbishing the church around 1620 (Pevsner 1989, 223). After his death the estate passed by marriage to the Stawell family. In 1689 John, the second Lord Stawell, inherited and began a rebuilding programme at Low Ham – 'a most sumptuous and expensive edifice' (Collinson

Figure 36
Low Ham, Somerset: air photograph of the garden site (RCHME, © Crown copyright).

60

1791, 444–6); but died on 30 November 1692, at the age of 24. Some thirty years after his death, the manor of Low Ham was purchased by the Phelips family, and thence descended to the Mildmays of Hazlegrove (Lankester 1958, 31).

The bulk of the physical remains at Low Ham lie to the south of the church in a rectangular field formerly called The Warren. Here are massive earthworks comprising a series of level garden terraces or parterres. These are separated by massive, steep scarps containing traces of stone revetment walling. The earthworks show clearly on air photographs and, sometimes, the buried wall footings are also visible (Fig 36).

Low Ham church forms a focus for the earthworks and is one of the keys to understanding them. It is described by Pevsner as:

remarkably compact in its proportions, the tower not high, the nave not long, and the clerestory tall...The tower is Somerset Perp standard......It is one of the most instructive cases of early Gothicism in England (Pevsner 1989, 223).

Indeed the church looks like a medieval Somerset church but in miniature. In reality, it was built mostly in the 1620s (with alterations in the 1660s). Its date, contrived appearance and position at the foot of the flight of garden terraces, and on the end of the principal vista through them, indicate that it was intended to be part of the overall garden design. It also served as a mausoleum and contains two main monuments: to Sir Edward Hext and his wife Dionysia; and to Sir Ralph Stawell.

The whereabouts of the mansion built or refurbished by Sir Edward Hext has been, and to some extent remains enigmatic but it was described by Collinson (1791, 444–6) as one of the finest in the west of England. It is not represented in the earthworks but by a process of identifying, interpreting and discounting other features, it has been possible to suggest its most likely position. The first clue is that Hext was responsible for much of the refurbishment of the church, and its appearance is probably largely due to him. Its purpose as an embellishment to the gardens is emphasised by its location at one end of a cutting or vista which runs up through the terraces. If the church lies at one end of the vista, what lay at the other? The house?

Secondly, the terraced gardens formed a rectangular block comprising all of the field, known later as The Warren, together with a wedge-shaped arrangement of terraces (now cut off from The Warren by a massive wall), to the east. Again the wedge arrangement, with an avenue along it (represented by tree-holes), points to the position of the great house at its southern end. It may be assumed, therefore, that Hext's mansion lay immediately south of the rectangular field.

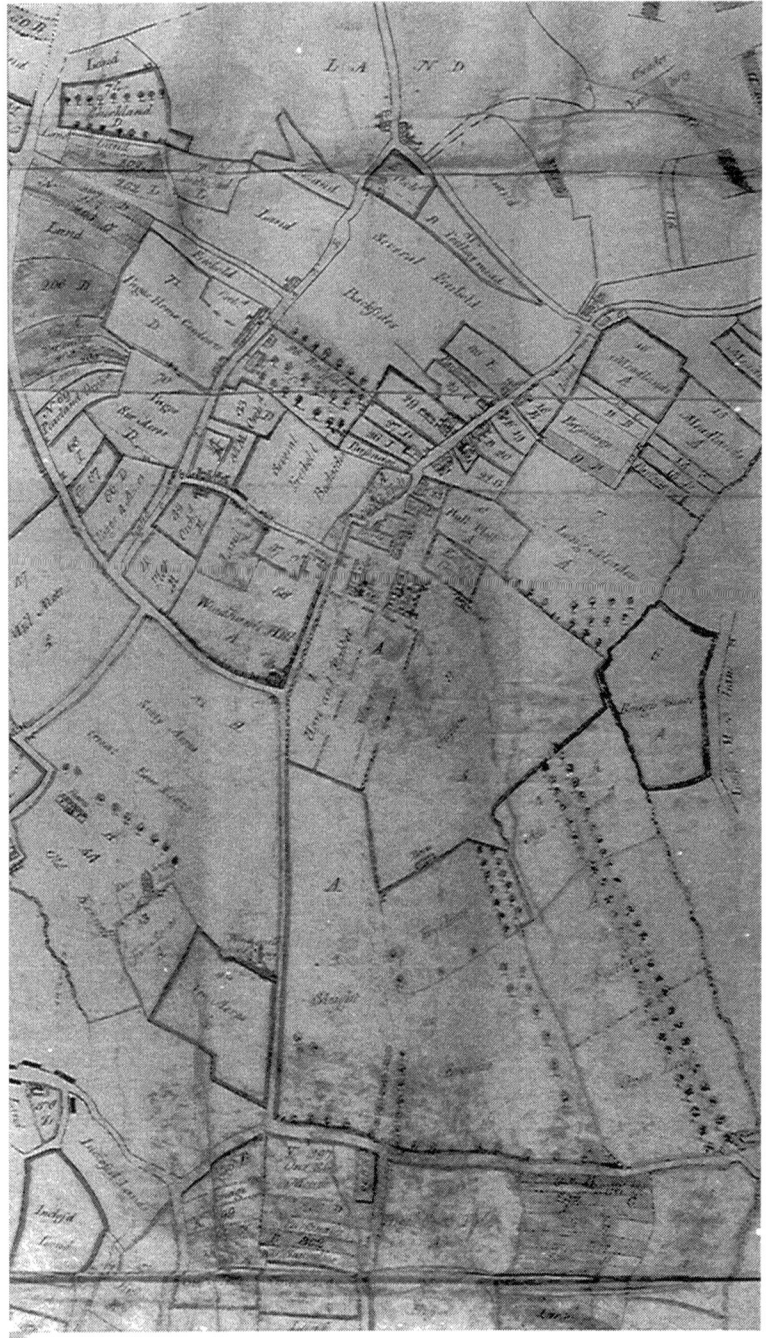

Future work, including geophysical survey, may confirm this interpretation and resolve its precise position.

The detailed layout of the gardens cannot be ascertained from the field evidence. They formed a roughly rectangular area, probably defined on the eastern side by an avenue of trees aligned on the house, and were dominated by a series of great terraces, revetted with limestone walling.

It had been suggested that the earthworks at Low Ham represented two successive gardens adjacent to one another and on slightly different alignments (Aston 1978, 26). This survey demonstrates instead that both were on the same alignment, and that Stawell intended to rework the

*Figure 37
Low Ham, Somerset:
extract of 1779 map,
showing avenues and
detail (reproduced by kind
permission of the Somerset
Archive and Record
Service; SRO DD/MKG
Box 4).*

central part of the Hext design, but that his death prevented the work from being completed. In 1689, Stawell began work on a great house to replace the Hext mansion: he had boasted that he would have the finest house, horse and wife in Somerset. Although he married Margaret, daughter of James Cecil, 3rd Earl of Salisbury at St John's College, Oxford in 1691, we know as little about his equestrian activities as we do of the great house he envisaged.

It was placed in a 'very low and bad situation' (Stawell 1910), and was left unfinished when Stawell died in 1692. Collinson (1791, 444–6), writing in the 1790s, describes it as:

vast piles of a stately ruin.....three rooms at the south end were finished and had very magnificent painted ceilings now dropping down to rubbish. The kitchen is inhabited by a farmer....

A map of 1779 (Fig 37; SRO DD/MKG Box 4: Map of Low Ham Estate by Samuel Donne) depicts the main elevation of the Stawell mansion, but in an unreliable, conventionalised form, and there is no other known depiction of it. Nevertheless, the house can be confidently located through a combination of topographic evidence and two plans, the one of 1779, the other of 1823 (SRO DD/SAS c/212: Map of Low Ham). It lay immediately to the east of the church, in an area now occupied by modern farm buildings and yards. Collinson (1791, 444–6) states that the house was 130 yards (119 m) long and 30 yards (27 m) wide. Moreover, there are three half-columns *in situ*, within a wall forming part of a slurry pit, which may have formed part of the internal face of the east wall of the house. Other architectural fragments from Stawell's great house are incorporated into later buildings. It would seem then, from the scant evidence available, that Stawell's mansion was rectangular in plan, some 27 m wide and probably around 70 m long.

Stawell had ambitious plans for the landscape setting of his mansion. To the east was an area of parkland, crossed by avenues, clearly shown on the 1779 map, and in places surviving as a combination of linear earthworks and tree holes. The short main drive approached from the west, where substantial gates are shown in 1779. The 1779 map also shows a number of features around the house: a walled cherry orchard, which survives today, and an L-shaped barn with what looks like a turret at one end (this building was replaced by a 19th-century barn, which follows its ground plan and is presumably built on its footings (Cattell 1996)).

The formal gardens in the immediate vicinity of the house were also to be reorganised. The house stood at the foot of a substantial flight of terraces, which formed part of the Hext gardens, stretching away to the south. Stawell built a massive limestone wall – up to 6m high, running southwards for 290 m – that cut across some of the lower garden terraces, and therefore excluded them from his scheme. To the west, within the field subsequently known as The Warren, he intended to rework the Hext gardens, a labour which he apparently began but never completed. The overall impression is one of unsatisfactory compromise, with the house squeezed into an existing arrangement and rightly described as in a 'low and bad situation'.

Part of the evidence for this unfinished scheme is contained in a letter written in 1690, either to Stawell or his steward, by Jacob Bobart (Stawell 1910, 424–5). Bobart was Superintendent of the Physic Garden at Oxford and one of the outstanding plantsman of his day. His letter is as follows:

First we suppose the Tarras walke to be the basis of the whole thence a perpendicular to arise to take the middle of the passage out of the house and from this line all the side walls to run parallel. The Tarras to be about 90 f [27.4 m] broad which may imperceptibly rise 6 or 8 inches [0.15 m or 0.2 m] from thence a paire of staires of 10 steps riseing 70 inches [1.77 m] which carries up to the first plot 262 f [79.8 m] square assending 168 inches [4.2 m]. Then ariseing 5 steps or 35 inches [0.88 m] up to the plot where the Canall is to be the plot 74 feet [22.5 m] with the Canall in the middle of the same 40 f [12.1 m] broad and 80 f [24.3 m] long (if it be concluded to be a parallelogram or whither an Octagonall figure would not keep cleaner considering there is noe great flux of water). From this plot arises another paire of staires of 10 steps 70 inches [1.77 m] which deliver you up to a plot of 260 f [79.2 m] square ascending 192 inches [4.8 m]. Then 10 steps more 70 inches [1.77 m] high carrying up to the Wilderness 260 f [79.2 m] square ascending allsoe 192 inches [4.8 m] The length of the whole with what the steps take up is about 980 feet [298.7 m] ascending 848 inches [21.5 m].

This information, despite being well known to previous researchers, had never been tested on the physical remains at Low Ham. When the measurements are superimposed over the earthwork survey (Fig 38), they coincide exactly with the overall length of the massive garden wall, which therefore must have been built by Stawell; they also correlate with some of the earthwork evidence. From this, it is clear that Bobart's letter refers to the central section of the gardens. The correlation between some of the lower terrace scarps, which are overlaid by Stawell's wall and those to the west of it that played a part in his gardens, confirms that the Bobart/Stawell scheme was a remodelling of Hext's terraces.

Because of Stawell's premature death, it is not clear whether this was the full extent of the planned garden. The area to the west, between the 1690s reworking and the road, contains well–made ter-

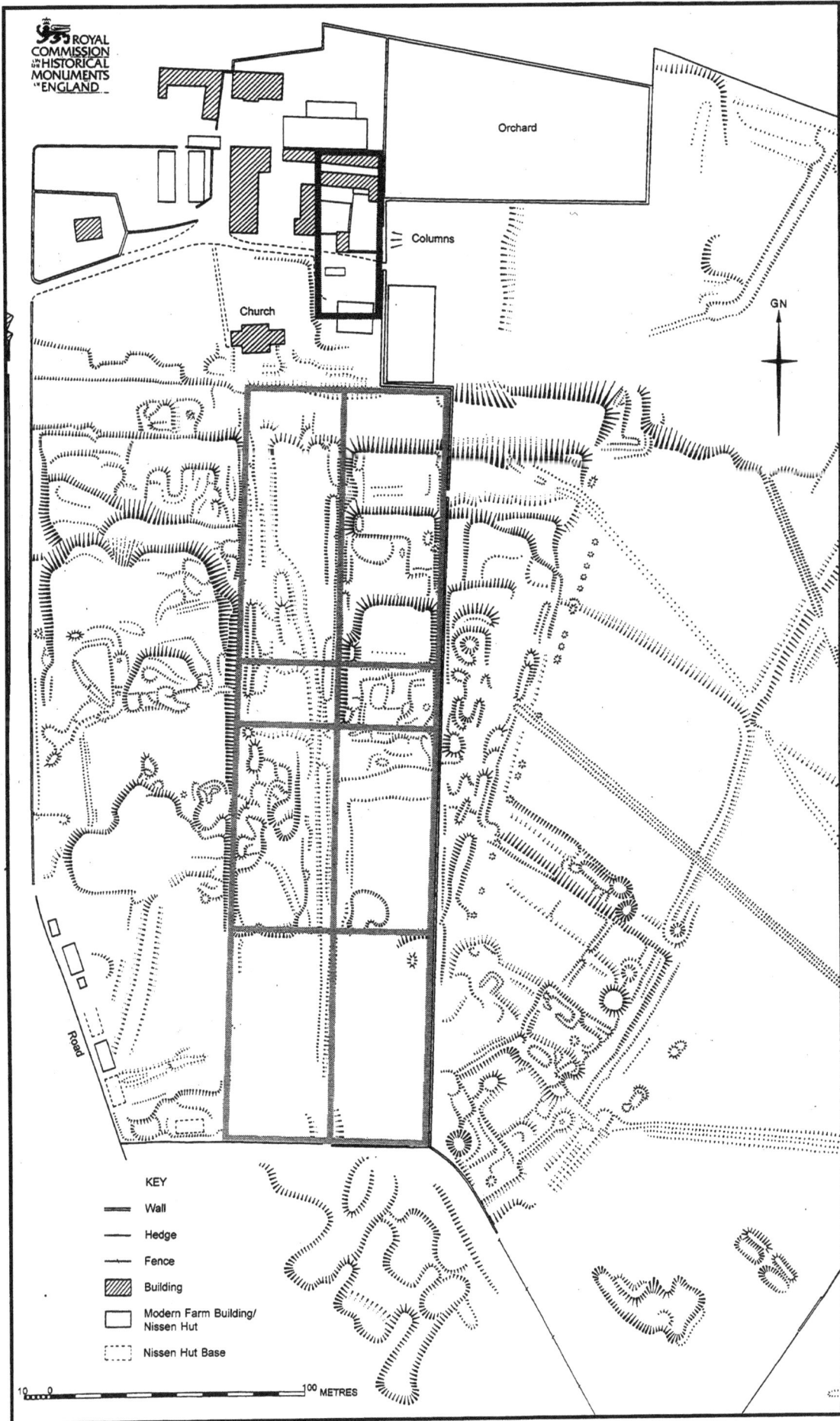

ROYAL
COMMISSION
ON THE
HISTORICAL
MONUMENTS
OF ENGLAND

Orchard

Columns

Church

GN

Road

KEY

Wall

Hedge

Fence

Building

Modern Farm Building/
Nissen Hut

Nissen Hut Base

10   0   100 METRES

Figure 38
*Low Ham,
Somerset:
earthwork plan
with Jacob Bobart's
measurements
superimposed
(RCHME, ©
Crown copyright).*

races at the lower end, but further up the hill these become amorphous dumps of material, rather like spoil heaps. It is possible that they represent garden terraces and other features under construction; perhaps dating to the 1690s and forming an unfinished extension to the Stawell design.

Bobart's measurements also confirm the position of the 1690s house, for the pronounced linear depression running down through the centre of the plots must be the 'perpendicular' arising out of 'the middle of the passage out of the house'. It can be assumed, therefore, that this ran straight to the centre of the south front (see Fig 38).

After Stawell's death, the house became a monstrous problem, and endured in the landscape for some time, until it finally mouldered away. Its demise is hinted at in various documents: a survey of 1722 (SRO DD/MKG 22) indicates that the Phelips family were uncertain what to do with it and, perhaps, that by this stage it had no value, for the survey is entitled: 'A survey Of the Manor and Demesnes of Netherham in the County of Somerset late the estate of John Lord Stawell deceased and which is to be sold with or without the great house.'

Collinson records that a farmer was living in part of the house by the 1790s. In 1823 there were only fragmentary ruined walls and by 1861 unintelligible piles of rubble marked the site (Anon 1861).

The terraced gardens suffered a similar fate, becoming a warren by the end of the 18th century, the great terraces making convenient burrows for rabbits. Subsequently, it reverted to farmland.

Low Ham's importance lies in the sequence which the earthworks represent, and the way in which the Hext layout was adapted at the end of the 17th century. Stawell's intention was essentially to turn the garden around: Hext's great house at the southern end was replaced by Stawell's mansion at the northern end. However, the complex earthwork sequence is difficult to disentangle, a situation exacerbated by our ignorance of the overall scheme which Stawell envisaged and even further complicated by the fact that the Stawell phase was unfinished. This last aspect of Low Ham further increases its importance, because encapsulated in the earthworks is a rare example of a 17th-century garden under construction.

CONCLUSIONS

What contribution do sites like Low Ham and Witham make to the study of garden history? At the most basic level, there is a powerful argument for ensuring that the recording and interpretation of the evidence which they contain is as sophisticated as possible. In both cases, the RCHME's recent surveys have significantly altered and refined the existing interpretations, providing new angles for garden historians, architectural historians, students of monastic history and other archaeologists to pursue. This has been possible through the accurate and detailed recording of the field evidence using appropriate non-invasive techniques, and by the subsequent application of good quality source material to that archaeological data.

Furthermore, the gardens at Witham and Low Ham form parts of a complex sequence of landscape development. They were influenced by the framework of what already existed, and equally, influenced what followed. As John Phibbs points out (this volume) for the 18th century, the concept of 'sweeping away' is in general much overplayed. This is encapsulated in the Jacob Bobart document which illustrates how he was working within an existing design. Even the position of Stawell's mansion was influenced by the earlier gardens but, perhaps surprisingly, the garden design was not compromised by the fact that it could be turned completely around, with the house shifting from one end to the other.

At Witham, this evolutionary process is again stressed. The Carthusian monastery influenced the position of the later house built from its ruins, and the monastic precinct defined the formal layout. Within it the Great Cloister became a privy garden. The striking open portico to Gibbs' house was complemented by a dramatic vista, hitherto unappreciated, which involved the moving of the River Frome to allow the construction of two lakes. By the end of the 18th century, Robert Adam's great drive was aligned on the monastic fabric entombed in the earlier house, a factor which no doubt would have influenced the development of the whole park if it had come to fruition.

Finally, the major contribution of the techniques described in this paper is that they are able to recover the plans and layout of short-lived gardens and to provide insights into the design aspirations of their creators. Equally, they enable these gardens to be understood, not as textbook exemplars of a particular style, but as more subtle and complex real creations, the product of their designers' and owners' sense of place.

ACKNOWLEDGEMENTS

I am grateful to various RCHME staff, too numerous to mention individually, for their contributions to the fieldwork, architectural analysis, air photography and air photographic transcriptions. I would especially like to thank Stephen Porter for providing so much of the architectural context, and for so much fruitful discussion.

The Somerset Archive and Record Service kindly gave permission for the reproduction of the 1779 map of Low Ham (Fig 37); the remaining illustrations were produced by Phil Newman.

The archived plans and site accounts are available for public consultation during normal office hours at the National Monuments Record Centre, Great Western Village, Kemble Drive, Swindon SN2 2GZ; telephone (01793) 414600, fax (01793) 414606.

A NEW FIELD OF WELSH CULTURAL HISTORY: INFERENCE AND EVIDENCE IN GARDENS AND LANDSCAPES SINCE *c* 1450

C Stephen Briggs

ABSTRACT

The quantitative and qualitative potential of historic gardens and parklands in Wales is outlined. A selective site-based history demonstrates changing fashions since medieval times. Methods of site investigation are considered, drawing upon work at a handful of recently investigated sites. It is argued that sites of all periods possess valuable historical research potential and are archaeologically sensitive. A growing impetus to manage or restore historic landscapes and gardens makes greater the urgency for systematic site and landscape survey and record.

INTRODUCTION

For many years Wales appeared not to be endowed with those classic medieval and later earthworks discovered, defined and surveyed in England, during the fieldwork which followed a greater understanding of deserted medieval villages (Taylor 1983b). And if the *Oxford Companion to Gardens* (1988) were to be believed, the Principality was almost bereft of those landscape fashions, which, for around five centuries, so fundamentally influenced demesnes on the English side of Offa's Dyke (Jellicoe *et al* 1988, 592). Until recently, Wales, it appeared, had suffered an aesthetic and functional provincialism, most of its landscape sheltered from the philosophies or will to change. How far is such a picture still justified?

MEDIEVAL AND LATER, PRIMITIVE OR FUNCTIONAL EARTHWORK SITES

Wales's landuse history is rendered the more interesting because its montane, agriculturally marginal land has suffered intermittent abandonments ever since the Bronze Age. In recent years, serious attempts to understand these processes have involved systematic archaeological survey, some of it undertaken through an Uplands Initiative funded by the Welsh Office through RCAHMW. It is clear that patterns of early gardening and evidence for primitive horticultural practice do survive around many undated upland – supposedly seasonal – steadings traditionally known as *hafotai*.

One group of earthworks, lying in the Ystwyth Forest, inland from Aberystwyth at Bwlch yr Oerfa, appears to have been a series of garden beds of considerable antiquity, possibly medieval (Briggs 1991, 240, fig 12.2). There is a similar site at Lan Fraith (SN 779 733; Fig 39), which was a farm marked upon Blake's plan of Hafod in 1796 (Cumberland 1796). It was probably abandoned around 1800. A number of comparable earthworks belonging to a broad spectrum of social and historical milieux are noted elsewhere in Wales (Briggs 1991, 138–44).

MONASTIC GARDENS AND VERNACULAR MEDIEVAL GARDENS

It was probably Hadrian Allcroft (1908, 453–93) who first outlined the wide variety of activity which could still be recognised within moated sites. Over several seasons' work, the Wood Hall Moated Manor Project (Womersley, N Yorks) has not only shown how the study of visible earthworks can be enhanced by excavation, but it is also demonstrating how apparently undistinguished sites may be rich in buried or waterlogged deposits, including pollen in early garden soils (Medieval Archaeology 39 (1995) 261–3; Medieval Settlement Research Group Annual Report 10 (1995), 36–8). It would be interesting to see the results of similar in-depth investigations at Welsh sites, not only within well-preserved earthworks like Horseland Moat (RCAHMW 1984,

Figure 39
*Lan Fraith,
Cwmystwyth,
Ceredigion: air
photo of an aban-
doned farm and its
garden beds
(RCAHMW, ©
Crown copyright).*

fig 44; Briggs 1991, 140–1, fig 12.3), but also upon some of the more anonymous Marcher moated sites.

The value of historic garden reconstruction is noted in Sylvia Landsberg's recent book on medieval gardens (Landsberg 1995). In Wales, an interesting wooden garden has been created at Tretower Court as an adjunct to the original 15th to 16th century court buildings.

Haverfordwest Priory

At present, some of the most comprehensive insights into medieval gardens are probably to be had from monastic sites, like the grange at Monknash in the Vale of Glamorgan (Briggs 1991, 139, fig 12.1; RCAHMW 1984, fig 144; Musson 1994, 37), and at other monastic sites (Briggs *idem* 139–40; Landsberg 1995 *passim*).

The best evidence so far unearthed illustrating medieval gardening in Wales comes from Haverfordwest's Augustinian Priory, excavated by Sian Rees (pers comm). In this garden complex, soil is roughly revetted by stone into nine square or rectangular plots of varying sizes on low-lying ground (Fig 40). Some are raised, and one enclosure appears to have been an arbour with a central square. All are in a form roughly similar to those depicted on some medieval manuscripts. In due course, soil samples are to be submitted for macro and micro-analysis to help gain a better understanding of their original role and product. The results of this work are awaited with interest.

RENAISSANCE GARDENS

Since architectural features of Renaissance style form an important component of Welsh gentry houses (Smith 1988), it is hardly surprising that many of Wales's gardens should have been similarly inspired by the European classical tradition.

Surviving minor gentry houses of the 15th and 16th centuries are relatively rare, the best examples of Renaissance architecture belonging to the great rebuilding of the 17th century. Most of the earlier structures are now incorporated into later dwellings, around which successive landscaping or farming practice has usually obliterated earlier evidence for horticultural activity. In 1937 the RCAHMW noted how traces of early plans of gardens were still to be found at a handful of 16th-century houses on the Isle of Anglesey (RCAHMW 1937, cliv). Among them were earthworks which still survive at Bodychen (*idem* 20), recently surveyed by Bangor undergraduates supervised by Frances Lynch. These earthworks (Fig 41) share similiarities with both older and some more recently abandoned garden features.

Renaissance garden earthworks comparable in scale to those of England (Taylor 1983b) have been noted at Landshipping (Fig 42) and Coedcanlas in Pembrokeshire. At Landshipping it is possible to pick out the sites of individual trees, whilst Coedcanlas possesses some remarkably regular enclosure plots of unknown function, which, at present, are difficult to parallel elsewhere.

66

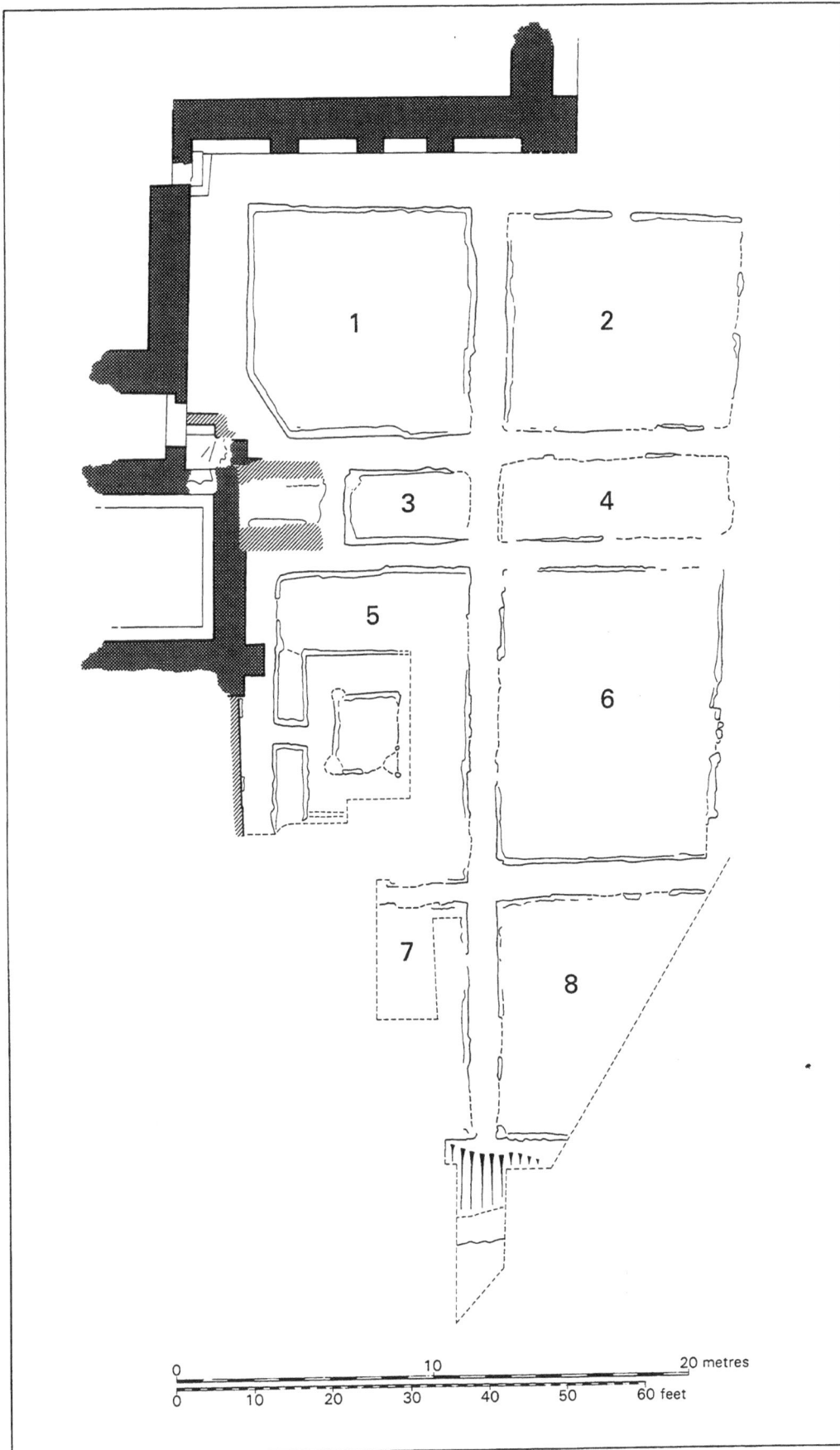

Figure 40 *Haverfordwest Priory, Pembrokeshire: garden beds (by kind permission of Sian Rees).*

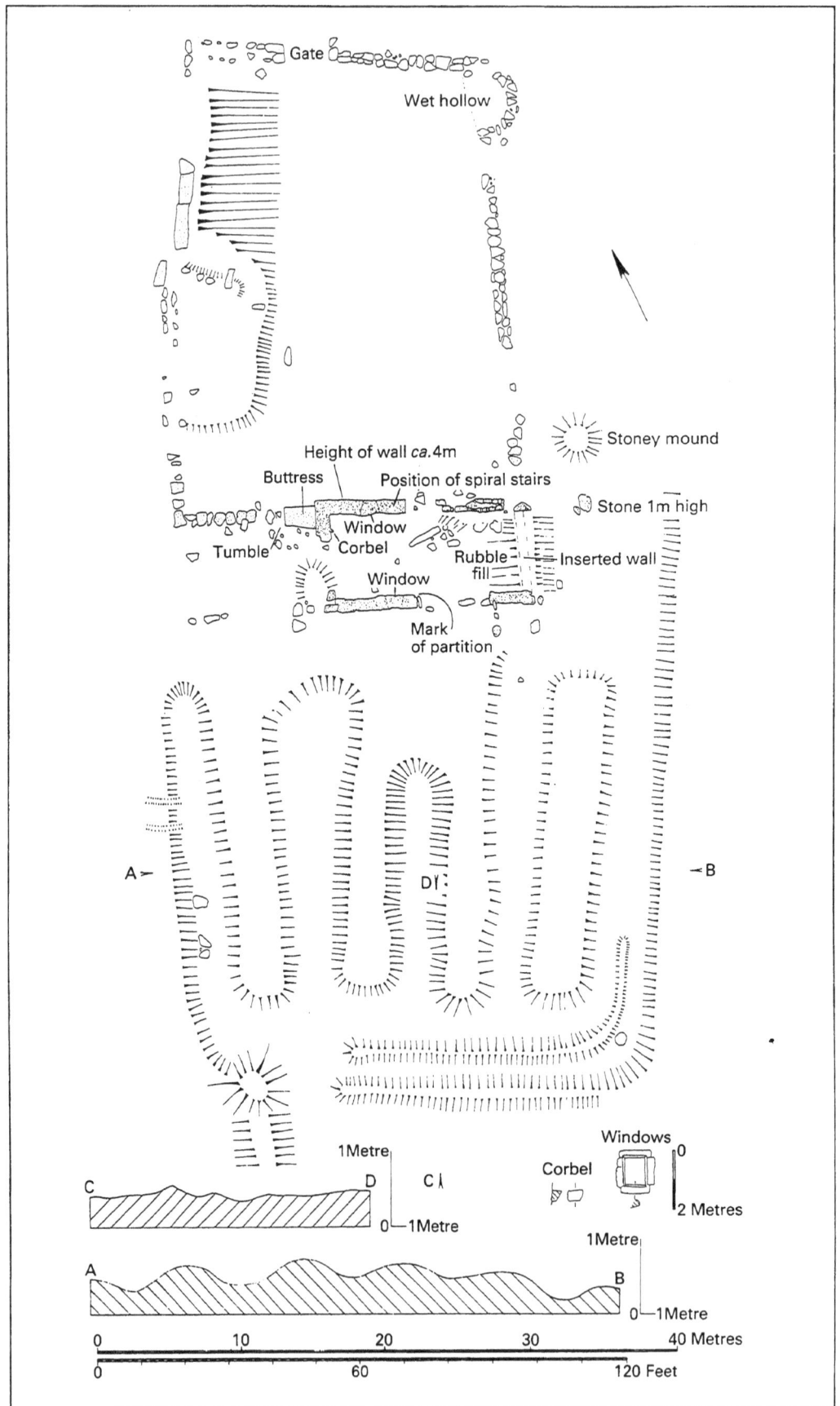

Figure 41 *Bodychen, Isle of Anglesey: plan of the garden beds, perhaps of 16th-century date (by kind permission of Frances Lynch).*

Figure 42
*Landshipping,
Pembrokeshire;
air photo of
the early
garden
features
(RCAHMW,
© Crown
copyright).*

Through the RCAHMW's joint long-term interest, with the Snowdonia National Park, in the palimpsest landscape around Dyffryn Ardudwy and Corsygedol in Merioneth, a GIS experiment was undertaken on Corsygedol's estate nucleus by overlaying an 18th-century estate plan onto digitised 25-inch plans (Fig 43). The plotting method threw up boundary location discrepancies which are only likely to be understood if the site is excavated. Nevertheless a valuable visual reconstruction of the site's development was created, based upon all known documents.

St Donat's Castle

Wales certainly had its share of courtiers and travellers familiar with high European, and more particularly, with Italian Renaissance fashion, men who were thus likely to have emulated it. One such individual was Sir Edward Stradling, the late 16th-century scholar owner and likely creator of gardens at St Donat's Castle, Vale of Glamorgan. He described them in Latin verse and his *Horti Sui Donataei Descriptio* lyrically lists the animals outside the walls and the plants within them. He effused how:

> *with its welcome covering a juicy vine clothes
> the wall around and makes it sacred to
> Bacchus. As a bracelet is an embellishment to
> the snow-white arms of an honest lady, as
> gold rings adorn tender fingers, and as a
> pearl shines out among cheaper stones, so too
> the early cluster of grapes gleam on the vine.*

His ode continues in fructitious vein, unfortunately without mentioning readily identifiable garden features (Davies 1981, 44–5).

The gardens at St Donat's still preserve terraced enclosures, even hanging gardens, stretching, Mediterranean-style, down to the sea. One of a growing number of terraced sites in Wales, mostly built into valley sides and surviving on a more modest scale (Briggs 1991, 143–4), the Stradling's Renaissance home amply illustrates the European dimension in contemporary Welsh courtly culture. Other recently recognised examples include Park and Maesypandy in Merioneth, at one time the homes of local dynastic land-owning families (Cato 1989, map opp 1).

Trawscoed

As has been noted elsewhere (Briggs 1991, 147), garden historians are fortunate in having Dineley's tour in Wales of 1684 to draw upon as a source for contemporary formal garden sketches (Banks 1888). Visiting the Vaughans' Trawscoed (Cardiganshire), Dineley indicated two successive formal enclosures which (though still detectable through aerial photography) later disappeared. These Vaughans severally held high office in Elizabethan and Jacobean government (Morgan 1997). Occupied by MAFF for much of the post-war period, in 1996 the estate was re-sold to the surviving Vaughan descendants who intend residential development on the site. Here, GIS historical mapping at RCAHMW illustrated an original 16th or 17th-century axial arrangement aligned north east to south west.

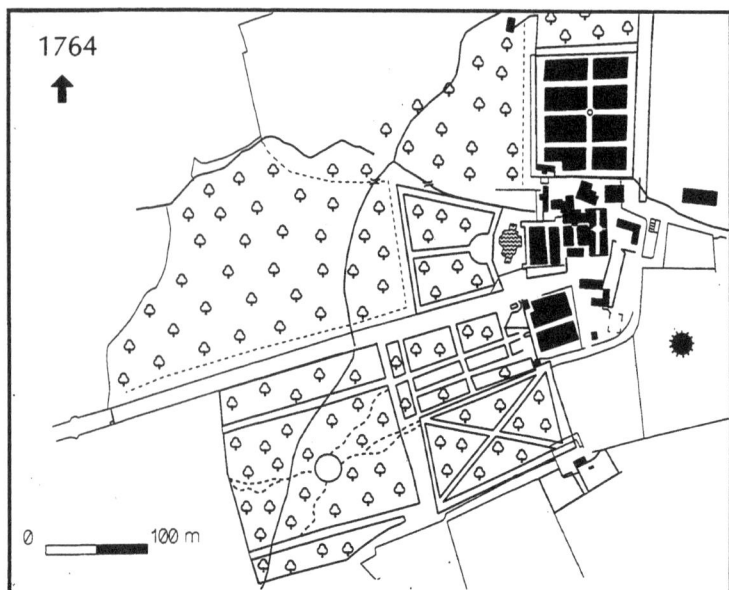

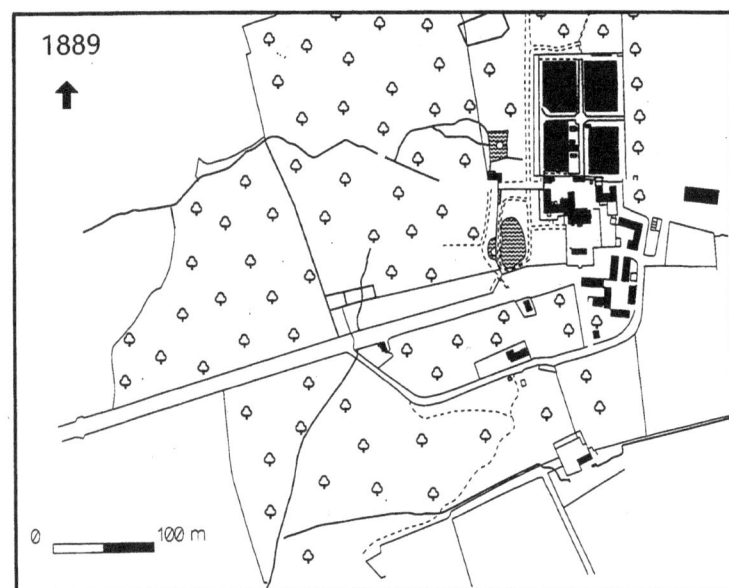

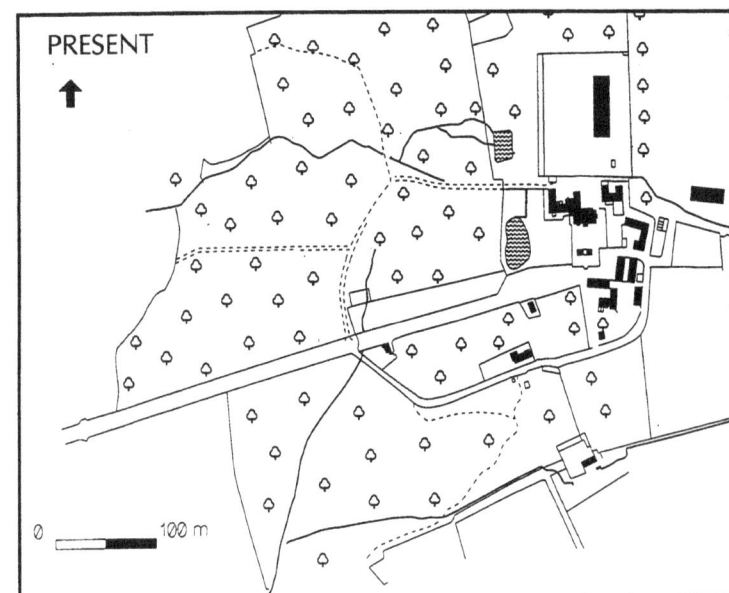

This shows how the house was approached from the north, down a now lost avenue-cum-carriage drive. It also demonstrates where the early formal enclosures were located; those on the south are now beneath a Victorian layout. This GIS plot has assisted Ceredigion County Planning Authority in its understanding of the site during planning consultations for the development proposals.

Old Gwernyfed

The architectural importance of Old Gwernyfed, lying between Brecon and Hay-on-Wye in the western foothills of the Black Mountains, has long been recognised (Haslam 1979, 319) through its designation as a Grade I listed building. Built by Williamses, well-placed in the Elizabethan court and Jacobean government, Old Gwernyfed's relatively unchanged state is owed to an 18th-century abandonment. Old Gwernyfed's surviving landscape includes earthworks which are amongst the most spectacular surviving Renaissance garden features in Wales. Particular interest attaches to this place because of the challenge it offers to equating the surviving features with elements in a poem describing complete refurbishment of both house and garden in 1604. Nesta Lloyd (pers comm) has translated, from local Welsh dialect, this contemporary wedding poem celebrating the union of its hereditary incumbent, Sir Harry Williams, with Eleanor Whitney from the nearby eponymous Herefordshire parish in that year. Its spirit is captured by the following quotation:

Welcome now lady, most able in Christendom, to Gwernyfed court:

And by that Court there is a garden of handsome plants, pure plants,

A meadow, a compact clean mile, of the finest under the crown;

On these there are flowers, the number of the dew falling in the morning;

Princes could stroll gracefully around the garden along each aisle

And your fine orchards are the place which bears white apples.

Costards like white sugar, quince and red corsling;

and every tasty thing that can grow on a live tree

Fine is the smallest part of the flower, splendid is the root that fails nothing.

Six or seven fish ponds without counting construction or greensward

Until they draw into them from every place the pure cold springs

Figure 43 *Corsygedol, Merioneth: GIS plots (RCAHMW, © Crown copyright).*

70

Detailing the new works to the family home, Williams's bard went on to explain elaborate and imaginative amenity plans for the entire estate, and it would be useful to establish how far these were undertaken.

This literary survival from the Welsh March pre-dates the genre of English Country House Poetry, as defined by Alastair Fowler (1994). Its discovery has helped reinvigorate interest in estate descriptions known to have been available in an earlier Welsh literary genre (Roberts 1986 *passim*). The value of these sources to medieval property and landscape descriptions is now being demonstrated more clearly through documentary searches by scholars at the Centre for Advanced and Celtic Studies, University of Wales.

Here, it is of more than passing interest that an archaeological evaluation of the site – undertaken in 1992 and commissioned under the provision of PPG 16 – ascertained the presence and extent of archaeologically interesting cultural deposits, quite close to the present-day ground surface (Thomas and Morriss 1993). One trench transected the top of a linear feature described by the excavators as a 'field drain'. Capped by stone slabs up to 1 m square, it seems likely that the investigators had hit one of the major feeders from Gwernyfed Commons to the water features in the Williams's Renaissance garden. Further investigation is obviously desirable.

Tredegar House

Even prior to their recent excavation and restoration, the formal walled gardens at Tredegar House, Newport (Gwent) might reasonably have been described as 'one of the most important early 18th-century garden landscapes in Wales' (Freeman 1990; Whittle 1993). Probably originally constituting a Tudor five-enclosure garden layout to the south west of the medieval house, in the early 1700s its garden walls were realigned and reconstructed in brick, rather than stone, to make three enclosures linked by one central gravel path, running parallel to the house.

The largest, most southerly enclosure contained the orchard and gardener's cottage with ancillary buildings. Next came the Cedar Garden, on its present pattern no more than a century old, but possibly originally laid out in the Dutch style, before becoming an American shrub garden in the late 18th century.

The third, northernmost enclosure, the Orangery Garden, was geophysically surveyed, then excavated, between 1989 and 1991 by the Debois Partnership (1989a; b: c; 1990; Ewart and Phibbs 1990). Unfortunately, the manuscript excavation plan offers limited clues as to the pattern of the original parterre, which the excavators felt had been surfaced 'with different coloured materials including sea shells, crushed lime mortar, brickdust, coal dust, white sand, yellow sand, orange sand and grass, all arranged in a formal pattern and sometimes bordered with low clipped box hedging'. It should be added that until this discovery, 'materials used for late 17th- and early 18th-century parterres were only known from contemporary garden writers' (Freeman 1990).

The site's very uniqueness is puzzling. However, whilst it is an attractive idea to attribute such a variety of coloured minerals to an otherwise unrecognised parterre-building tradition, it would not be difficult to explain most of them with reference to household activities. The presence of coal dust could relate to the heating of the orangery; the brickdust and mortar to aspects of rebuilding or fabric destruction; the sea shells to discarded table delicacies, and other coloured sands to local soil or geological process or anomaly. In spite of the potential importance of this site, apparently no soil samples have been submitted for laboratory examination, so it is impossible to compare either building, horticultural or design processes with the more comprehensive treatment afforded the roughly contemporary Privy Garden at Hampton Court (Dix 1995).

In spite of these many unresolved questions, the discoveries made in excavation resulted in a re-creation of imaginative parterres, designed to reflect the period *c* 1680–1800 (but with the idea of Dutch parterres uppermost). As experimental archaeology, this is an interesting, not to say, courageous departure; visually the result is attractive and exciting (though extremely difficult to maintain). A published account of the excavation is awaited with interest.

18TH–CENTURY GARDENS

Several (sometimes conflicting) landscape philosophies characterised or challenged 18th-century estate design and management. Ranging in style from the intricately formal to near-totally naturalistic, their great scale and complexity can make them daunting survey projects. Curiously, whatever may have been the intended aesthetic impact of planting programmes on the great 18th and 19th-century estates it is now often ancillary works, like aqueducting (such as survives at Middleton Hall (Ludlow 1995)), drainage (for example at Leighton Park), and workshops (like those surviving at Wynnstay), which demand most resource in field investigation.

Wilderness Picturesque Landscapes: Hafod

Created by Colonel Thomas Johnes between 1783 and 1815, Hafod is a demesne with no house, but this absence detracts little from its importance. Most interest attaches to its surviving, relatively unspoilt natural aspect, tribute to the landscape philosophy of its creator. Serious attempts at conservation here go back to 1985 (Briggs and Kerkham 1988; Kerkham and Briggs 1991). The site is at present the subject of a restoration project sponsored jointly between the Hafod Trust (formed in 1994), and Forest Enterprise who own the land.

Johnes's circuit walks originally led limited numbers of visitors along informal, sometimes ill-defined and probably unsurfaced routes (Hayden 1996–7), offering an introduction to the valley's wilderness qualities. Current proposals to redefine and open these routes, some surviving beneath post-war commercial afforestation, offers the challenge to strike a balance between increased visitor access and potential erosion of the historic environment (Briggs 1996–7a). Extensive excavations were undertaken under contract in 1994 (Briggs and Kerkham 1995) and more recently by Cambria, formerly the Dyfed Archaeological Trust (Murphy and Ramsey 1996), which has now been commissioned to establish a sites and monuments database and GIS for management purposes. As so few man-made structures or woodland stratigraphies can be recognised, post-excavation laboratory work on soils and pollen is still desirable.

Llanaeron

Llanaeron was bequeathed to the National Trust by the late Major Lewes in 1989–91. A modest gentry house of classical pretension, the novelty of its layout of *c* 1800, by John Nash, was estate-activity planning around rectangular yards spatially balanced by two adjacent large, walled, kitchen gardens. Farming was partially separated from gardening by a frameyard, boiler house, potting shelters and gardeners' accommodation (Suggett 1995).

Much enthusiastic activity by volunteers initially resulted in unresearched restoration of the walled gardens. Later, the site of an Edwardian rose garden, formerly in the north-western corner of the West Garden enclosure, was carefully excavated, deturfed, cleaned and planned. In 1996 roses were once more restored to it.

Two resident archaeologists were appointed in 1992, and a full EDM survey then made of the site (Ede and Mayes 1994). They were succeeded in 1995 by Nicky Evans, who made a thorough study of the surviving glasshouse structures in their various states of disrepair, preparatory to restoration. An example of her drawings (which are important models for recording in kitchen gardens), are illustrated here (Fig 44). They dem-

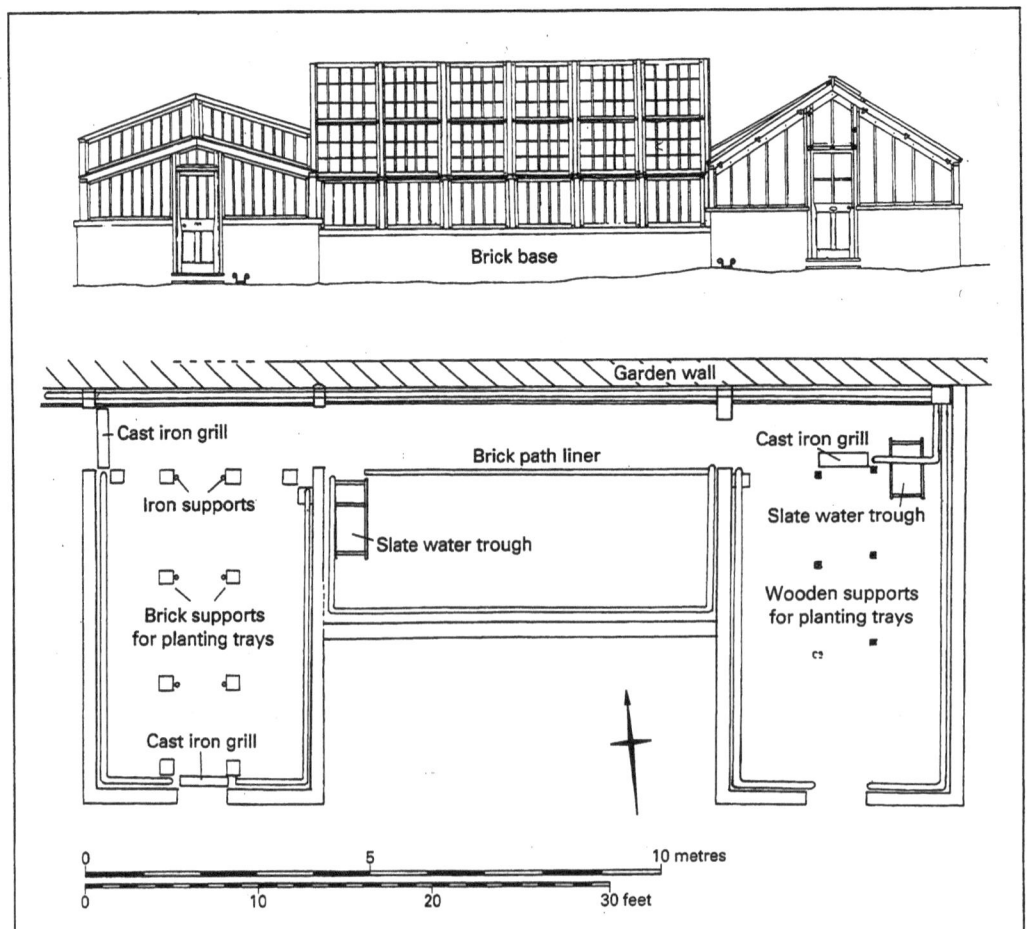

Figure 44
Llanaeron: greenhouses (by kind permission of Nicky Evans).

72

onstrate the value of detailed recording in kitchen gardens, where, as Susan Campbell (1985) notes, there remain many important unwritten chapters of garden history.

19TH-CENTURY AND LATER GARDENS: ABERGLASNEY

Aberglasney is an abandoned estate nucleus at Llangathen, near Llandeilo. The site possesses a raised 'walkway', a peculiar 'gothic' archway too narrow to have admitted a carriage, a pond, and until recently, the remains of a kitchen garden. The place has attracted interest because of its connection with the poet and artist John Dyer (Joyner 1995) and his landscape poetry of the 1720s focusing on nearby Grongar Hill. Besides this, the conclusions of a recent study (Samuels and Dixon-Hunt 1991) afford Aberglasney an important place in Welsh, if not in British 16th-century Renaissance gardens.

Interestingly, an expansive antiquarian tradition has evolved since Edwardian times, holding that a yew tunnel in front of the house is one thousand years old and that the cloistered court was built by Bishop Anthony Rudd around 1600. Investigating for the RCAHMW (1960s–1980s), however, P Smith and A J Parkinson have felt it unlikely that this feature, which resembles a row of limekilns, had been built much before c 1800. Although Wales does possess one walkway with an undoubted Renaissance pedigree in Llantrithyd Place (RCAHMW 1981, 175a–181b), there is little to compare the quality of cultural milieux, scale or functions between Llantrithyd and the walkway at Aberglasney.

Little is known of Bishop Rudd and detailed investigations into the background of the estate hardly support either Elizabethan or Jacobean dating, or the early importation of exotic Continental features (Briggs 1996). Disappointingly, archaeology has been of limited assistance in clarifying the historical record. Excavations were first undertaken here in 1961; Geophysical Surveys of Bradford (1991) and Lesley Howes (1992) each made independent surveys, then the Dyfed Archaeological Trust excavated in 1995 (Purdue et al 1995). None of these investigations have been able to confirm the existence of surviving stratigraphies or convincing in situ artefact assemblages earlier than the later 18th century. Although it has been proposed that the lake was a key feature of the Renaissance landscape (Samuels and Dixon-Hunt 1991), the basin was unfortunately recently cleaned out without reference to its palynological historical potential. If the site's inconclusive history is to be successfully unravelled, more detailed archaeological investigation will need to be involved in future remedial, conservation and restoration work.

DISCUSSION

Wales has a great number of historic gardens, many with important remains both above and below the ground. Monitoring by record and survey in advance of changing management regimes, through existing statutory and non-statutory planning procedures, is now variously shared by the limited resources of RCAHMW, Cadw, CCW, the WHGT, and the GHS. All are committed to working in partnership to achieve greater nationwide understanding of landscape development.

The RCAHMW is charged with recording and interpreting sites and landscape monuments, providing information and promoting a greater appreciation of their value. Although at present it is difficult to assess how many historic gardens exist and require survey, core data are available on around 2,000 gardens, mainly taken from desk-top map and aerial photographic research. If a significant number of 'those [earthwork] gardens associated with smaller houses and cottages' noted by Murphy (1997, 544) were to be added, that figure could easily be doubled or trebled. At present, most site visiting, which tends to be to minor gentry house gardens, is undertaken by members of the Welsh Historic Gardens Trust. Only a handful of EDM archaeological surveys have been commissioned under contract for the Commission since 1994.

When discussing Historic Garden Registration in Wales, Murphy also notes the 'current fashion for restoring and developing historic parks and gardens, often with inadequate research.' He goes on to suggest that 'the current [Cadw] register provides the prospective developer/restorer with a guide to the best sites with no built-in system of consultation, balances and checks', a situation needing to be 'amended if we are not to see much of the evidence of our historic gardens and parks rapidly disappear' (Murphy 1997, 544).

In this regard it is noteworthy that when, in 1995, a list of twenty-two sites was drawn up for consideration as a National Botanic Garden – including important historic sites like Glynllifon, Bodnant, Erddig, Bodelwyddan, Powis Castle, Middleton Hall, Clyne Gardens, Margam Park, Dyffryn, St Fagans, Bute Park, Tredegar Park, Ebbw Vale National Garden Festival Site, Tredegar Park, Wentwood, Piercefield House and Buckland Hall – the consultants considered virtually every aspect of access and development, except potential impact upon the historic environment or the archaeological resource. Therefore the need for, or value of, desktop assessment, research, survey and record prior to any intended change was not identified (Eres 1995, 4.6).

The Ebbw Vale Garden Festival site well illustrates the usefulness of pre-development or restoration evaluation. When the site was being developed between 1990 and 1992, an impression was given that a completely new country park was being created from the dereliction of an industrial wasteland. But historical investigation reveals that this was only partially the case. In fact the Ebbw Vale Country Park overlies the site of an earlier park around Victoria House, the Ebbw Vale ironworks manager's house of 1851. This comprised:

> '23 acres in which snipe and other game were strictly preserved, a fishpond of 1½ acres, an ice-house, lawns and ornamental gardens. Rebuilt in 1881 because of subsidence, it was abandoned in 1899 for the same reason, and in time the park was overwhelmed by great heaps of colliery waste and furnace slag which have long since buried its lawns and trees'(Jones 1970, 269).

Examination of the early 25-inch plans clearly shows that all did not disappear, however, and curiously, the Victorian pond and kitchen garden eventually corresponded with structural features integrated within the Garden Festival site. A more comprehensive survey and interpretation of Ebbw Vale's landscape history could easily have been incorporated into the ambitious plans which made this site such an important contribution to new urban parkland landscaping.

A final point about non-intrusive archaeological survey, already touched upon in discussion of moated sites, is that whilst it is vital to measure those features still visible above the ground, it is equally important to anticipate what may lie below it. Buried deposits hiding stratified cultural debris or plant, seed and pollen rich deposits, are in themselves a form of archive, demanding management, if not also protection. Ideally, these need assessment in parallel with architectural and earthwork mensuration (as is illustrated, for example, in Dix 1995). Silted-up lakes and watercourses are particularly vulnerable, since stratified silts could offer the only available clues to early plantings, landuse and vegetational history (Murphy and Wiltshire 1994). Ironically, at present, Jacobean, Georgian and Victorian vegetational or planting histories are probably less well understood in some parts of Britain than is the Neolithic Landnam Horizon (early forest clearing for farming) of the fourth millennium

BC. All reconnaissance techniques – topographical survey, photographic record, field and laboratory sampling work – need to go hand in glove to ensure a full understanding of both fugitive and well-preserved sites, particularly those which may be under threat.

CONCLUSION

It was noted, in introducing this paper, that in some circles Wales was felt to have lagged behind the landscape ideas which had so affected the rest of Britain since the Renaissance. Obviously a notion owed to limited intellectual inquiry, it has been shown that this image of provincialism is now changing dramatically. Recent years have seen several important institutional achievements as well as the historic surveys and investigations summarised here: the establishment of a Welsh Historic Gardens Trust in 1989 (Haslam 1990); the public commitment to a Cadw/ICOMOS Gardens Register (Cadw 1994; 1995) and creation of a database as part of the Extended National Database at RCAHMW, where the discovery and recognition of garden earthworks is also being addressed by some field recording (Briggs 1991). These are all signs of growing enthusiasm and appreciation of Wales's historic landscape resource. More published information has been made available about visitable Welsh historic gardens (for example, the Cadw/ICOMOS Gardens Register), whilst garden and parkland history is achieving a recognised role in estate and family histories (for example, Morgan 1997, 162–80). Concerns are being articulated about conservation, management and the protection of historic gardens through the planning process (Harden 1997), and recording, whether by aerial reconnaissance, from map and documentary research or topographical survey, is now being used to better help appreciate these several processes.

ACKNOWLEDGEMENTS

The writer thanks both his colleagues at RCAHMW and a number of correspondents for their assistance in producing this paper. Thanks are also due to Dr Nesta Lloyd for permission to quote from her unpublished translation of Sir Harry Williams's Wedding Poem. This contribution appears by permission of the Chairman, Secretary and Commissioners of the RCAHMW.

BIBLIOGRAPHY

Alexander B (ed), 1957 *Life at Fonthill, 1807–1822 ... from the correspondence of William Beckford*.

Allcroft A H, 1908 *Earthwork of England: Prehistoric, Roman, Saxon, Danish, Norman, and Medieval* Macmillan, London.

Allison K, 1957 'The Sheep-Corn Husbandry of Norfolk in the Seventeenth and Eighteenth Centuries' *Agricultural History Review* **5**, 12–38.

Anon, 1834 'Notes on gardens and Country Seats' *Gardening Magazine* **10**, 246–59.

1861 'Notes on Excursion' *Somerset Archaeology and Natural History* **11**, 24.

Ashbee P, 1972 'Field archaeology, its origins and development' in P J Fowler (ed) *Archaeology and the Landscape* John Baker, London.

Aspinall A and Pocock J A, 1995 'Geophysical prospection in garden archaeology: an appraisal and critique based on case studies' *Archaeological Prospection* **2**, 61–84.

Aston M A, 1970–72 'Earthworks at the bishop's palace, Alvechurch, Worcestershire' *Transactions of the Worcestershire Archaeological Society* **3rd ser 3**, 55–9.

1978 'Gardens and Earthworks at Hardington and Low Ham' *Somerset Archaeology and Natural History* **122**, 11–28.

Banks R W (ed), 1888 *Thomas Dineley's Account of the Official Progress through Wales of Henry, Duke of Beaufort in 1684* Blades, London.

Baring H (ed), 1866 *The Diary of the Right Honourable William Windham 1784–1810* London.

Barratt G, 1994 *Clun Castle, Shropshire* (English Heritage schedule entry).

Barrett J C, 1994 *Fragments from Antiquity: an Archaeology of Social Life in Britain 2900–1200 BC* Blackwell, Oxford.

Beaudry M, 1993 *Documentary Archaeology in the New World* Cambridge University Press, Cambridge.

Bettey J H, 1993 *Estates and the English Countryside* Batsford, London.

Bevan B W, 1994 'The magnetic anomaly of a brick foundation' *Archaeological Prospection* **1**, 93–104.

Bilikowski K, 1983 *Hampshire Countryside Heritage: Historic Parks and Gardens* Hampshire County Council.

Blood N K and Taylor C C, 1992 'Cawood: an archiepiscopal landscape' *Yorkshire Archaeological Journal* **64**, 83–102.

Bold J with Reeves J, 1988 *Wilton House and English Palladianism: Some Wiltshire Houses* HMSO, London.

Bond J and Iles R, 1991 'Early Gardens in Avon and Somerset' in A E Brown (ed) *Garden Archaeology* CBA Research Report **78**, 36–52.

Bonney D J and Dunn C J 1989, 'Earthwork castles and settlement at Hamstead Marshall, Berkshire' in M Bowden, D Mackay and P Topping (eds) *From Cornwall to Caithness; some aspects of British field archaeology, papers presented to Norman V Quinnell* BAR British Series **209**, 173–82.

Bradley R, 1996 'Re-thinking the later Bronze Age' in O Bedwin (ed) *The Archaeology of Essex* Essex County Council, Chelmsford.

Briggs C S, 1991 'Garden Archaeology in Wales' in A E Brown (ed) *Garden Archaeology* CBA Research Report **78**, 138–59.

1996 'Aberglasney and its landscape: interpreting the evidence' (Unpublished typescript in the National Monuments Record (Wales)).

1996-97a 'Conserving Hafod's Wilderness Picturesque' *Friends of Hafod Newsletter* **14**, 1–5.

Briggs C S, 1996-97b 'The Historic Gardens Database' *Gerddi* **1i**, 26–35.

Briggs C S and Kerkham C R, 1988 'Hafod' *Archaeology in Wales* **28**, 77–8.

1995 'Archaeology at Hafod in 1994: A Comment' *Friends of Hafod Newsletter*.

Brown A E and Taylor C C, 1973 'The gardens at Lyveden, Northants' *Archaeological Journal* **129**, 154–60.

1977 'Cambridgeshire earthworks surveys II' *Proceedings of the Cambridge Antiquarian Society* **64**, 90–2.

1991 'A relict garden at Linton, Cambridgeshire' *Proceedings of the Cambridge Antiquarian Society* **80**, 62–7.

Burrow I C G and Burrow C, 1990 'Witham Priory: The First English Carthusian Monastery' *Somerset Archaeology and Natural History* **134**, 141–82.

Butler L A S, 1987 'Holt Castle, John de Warenne and Chastellion', in J R Kenyon and R Avent (eds) *Castles in Wales and the Marches. Essays in honour of D J Cathcart King*, 106–24. University of Wales Press, Cardiff.

Cadw/ICOMOS, 1994 *Register of Landscapes, Parks and Gardens of Special Historic Interest in Wales: Part I: Parks and Gardens of Gwent* Cadw: Welsh Historic Monuments, Cardiff.

1995 *Register of Landscapes, Parks and Gardens of Special Historic Interest in Wales: Part I: Parks and Gardens of Clwyd* Cadw: Welsh Historic Monuments, Cardiff.

Campbell C, 1725 *Vitruvius Britannicus* privately published in three volumes, London.

Campbell S, 1985 'A Few Guidelines for the Conservation of Old Kitchen Gardens' *Garden History* **13**, 68–74.

Cato M K W, 1989 *Old Blood of Merioneth: A short History of the Nanney-Wynn Family and their Estates over Ten Centuries* Gomer Press, Llandyssul.

Cattell J, 1996 *Low Ham* (RCHME draft architectural notes, in the National Monuments Record).

Charlton B and Day J, 1984 'Henry MacLauchlan: surveyor and field archaeologist' in R Miket and C Burgess (eds) *Between and Beyond the Walls: Essays on the Prehistory and History of North Britain in Honour of George Jobey*, 4–37. John Donald Publishers Ltd, Edinburgh.

Cherry J, 1969 'The Dunstable swan jewel' *Journal of the British Archaeological Association*, **3rd ser 32**, 38–53.

Clarkson C, 1821 *The History of Richmond in the County of York* Privately published, Richmond.

Cobbett W, 1853 (1912 edition) *Rural Rides* volume **1** Dent, London.

Cole M A, David A E U, Linford N T, Linford P K and Payne A W, 1997 'Non-Destructive techniques in English Gardens: Geophysical Prospecting' *Garden History* **17**, 26–39.

Collinson Rev J, 1791 *The History and Antiquities of the County of Somerset*.

Colvin H M (ed), 1963 *The History of the King's Works* **2** *The Middle Ages* HMSO, London.

1982 *The History of the King's Works* **4** *1485–1660* **pt 2** HMSO, London.

Corbett G S, 1994 *Whorlton Castle Gatehouse, Whorlton, North Yorkshire* (RCHME Historic Building Report no. 86643, in the National Monuments Record).

Coulson C, 1992 'Some analysis of the castle of Bodiam, East Sussex' in *The Ideals and Practice of Medieval Knighthood* Proceedings of the Strawberry Hill Conference **4**, 51–107.

Crawford O G S, 1922 *The Andover District: An Account of Sheet 283 of the Ordnance Survey map* Oxford University Press.

1953 *Archaeology in the Field* Dent, London.

Cumberland G, 1796 *An attempt to Describe Hafod* Egerton, London.

Currie C, 1992 'St Cross: a medieval moated garden?' *Journal of the Hampshire Gardens Trust* **11**, 19–22.

David A, 1995 *Geophysical survey in archaeological field evaluation* English Heritage, London.

Davies C, 1981 *Latin Writers of the Renaissance* Cardiff University Press on behalf of the Welsh Arts Council.

Debois, 1989a *Tredegar House Gardens: Proposed Archaeological Survey* (Unpublished typescript presented to Newport Borough Council).

Debois, 1989b *A Survey of the Ornamental garden* (Unpublished typescript presented to Newport Borough Council).

1989c *Tredegar House Gardens: Archaeological Survey Findings* (Unpublished typescript presented to Newport Borough Council)

1990 *Report on Archaeological Survey* (Unpublished typescript presented to Newport Borough Council).

Dent J, 1981 *The Quest for Nonsuch* London Borough of Sutton Leisure Services.

Dix B, 1995 'The Excavation of the Privy Garden', in S Thurley (ed) *The King's Privy Garden at Hampton Court Palace 1689–1995*, 79–118. Apollo, London.

Dixon-Hunt J and Willis P (eds), 1988 *The Genius of the Place: The English Landscape Garden 1620–1820* The MIT Press, Cambridge Massachusetts/London.

Douglas Rev J, 1793 *Nenia Britannica*.

Dunlop G D, 1940 *Pages from the History of Highclere, Hampshire* Holywell Press, Oxford.

Ede J and Mayes I, 1994 *Llanerchaeron Park and Garden Survey: Draft Report* The National Trust.

Emery A, 1996 *Greater Medieval Houses of England and Wales 1300–1500* **1** *Northern England* Cambridge University Press.

English Heritage, 1984 *Register of Parks and Gardens of Special Historic Interest* **19** *Hampshire*.

1985 *Register of Parks and Gardens of Special Historic Interest* **39** *Suffolk*.

1987a *Register of Parks and Gardens of Special Historic Interest* **4** *Buckinghamshire*.

1987b *Register of Parks and Gardens of Special Historic Interest* **46** *Wiltshire*.

Eres, 1995 *National Botanic Garden for Wales: Feasibility Study Summary Report* (Report prepared for the Welsh Office).

Everson P, 1989 'The Gardens of Campden House, Chipping Campden, Gloucestershire' *Garden History* **17 pt 2**, 109–21.

1991 'Field survey and garden earthworks' in A E Brown (ed) *Garden Archaeology* CBA Research Report **78**, 6–19.

1995 'The Munstead Wood survey' in M Tooley and P Arnander (eds) *Gertrude Jekyll, Essays on the Life of a Working Amateur*, 71–82. Michaelmas Books, Witton-le-Wear.

1996a 'Bodiam Castle, East Sussex: castle and designed landscape' *Château Gaillard: études de castellologie médiévale* **16**, 79–84.

1996b 'The after-life of monastic houses: the earthwork evidence' in C Sturman (ed) *Lincolnshire People and Places: Essays in Memory of Terence R Leach* Society for Lincolnshire History and Archaeology, Lincoln.

1996c 'Bodiam Castle, East Sussex' in D M Evans, P Salway and D Thackray (eds) *The Remains of Distant Times*, 66–72 Society of Antiquaries of London Occasional Paper **19**.

Everson P, Taylor C and Dunn C J 1991 *Change and Continuity: Rural Settlement in North-West Lincolnshire* Royal Commission on the Historical Monuments of England/HMSO, London.

Ewart G and Phibbs J, 1990 *Excavation of the Orangery Garden at Tredegar House, 22–28 May 1990* (Unpublished typescript from the Debois partnership for Newport Borough Council).

Fear H J, 1961–3 'Westcombe' *Transactions of the Greenwich and Lewisham Antiquarian Society* **7.1**, 8–13.

Fowles J (ed) 1982, *John Aubrey: Monumenta Britannica* Dorset Publishing Company, Dorset.

Fowler A, 1994 *The Country House Poem: A Cabinet of Seventeenth Century Estate Poems and Related Items* Edinburgh University Press.

Freeman D, 1990 *The Orangery Garden* (Unpublished typescript on Tredegar Park).

1992 *The Gardens at Tredegar House* (Unpublished typescript).

Gaffney C, 1994 *Witham, Somerset. Geophysical Survey report* Geophysical Surveys of Bradford.

Geophysical Surveys of Bradford, 1991 *Report on Geophysical Survey: Aberglasney, Dyfed,* (Unpublished survey for the Welsh Historic Gardens Trust).

Greeves T A P, 1992 *Richmond Park: Archaeological Survey* (Report prepared for the Royal Parks Agency).

1993 *Bushy Park: Archaeological Survey* (Report prepared for the Royal Parks Agency).

Hadfield M, 1960 *Gardening in Britain (An Historical Outline)* Hutchinson, London.

Harden B (ed), 1997 'Towards the Millennium: The Conservation of Welsh Parks, Gardens and Designed Landscapes for the 21st Century' Report of a Conference held on Thursday 19th October 1995 at Plas Gogerddan, Aberystwyth, *Gerddi Journal of Welsh Historic Gardens Trust* **1:i**.

Hare J N, 1988 'Bishop's Waltham Palace, Hampshire: William of Wykeham, Henry Beaufort and the transformation of a medieval episcopal palace' *Archaeological Journal* **145**, 222–54.

Harris E, 1971 'The architecture of Thomas Wright' (3 parts) *Country Life* **150**, 492–5, 546–50 and 612–15.

Haselgrove C C, Turnbull P and Fitts R L, 1990 'Stanwick, North Yorkshire, part 1: recent research and previous archaeological investigations' *Archaeological Journal* **147**, 1–15.

Haslam R, 1979 *The Buildings of Wales: Powys* Penguin Books, London/University of Wales Press.

1990 'Order in the Wilds' *Country Life* **184**, 11 Jan 1990, 56–7.

Hatcher J, 1990 *Richmondshire Architecture* Privately published, Richmond.

Hayden P, 1996–97 'Paths in Picturesque Parks: some contemporary advice' *Friends of Hafod Newsletter* **14**, 16–18.

Holderness B A, 1972 '"Open" and "Closed" Parishes in England in the Eighteenth and Nineteenth Centuries' *Agricultural History Review* **20**, 126–39.

1984 'East Anglia and the Fens' in J Thirsk (ed) *The Agrarian History of England and Wales* **5 pt I**, 197–238.

Hoppitt, R 1992 A study of the development of parks in Suffolk from the eleventh to the seventeenth centuries (Unpublished PhD thesis, University of East Anglia).

Howes L, 1992 Aberglasney House, Parapet Structure, Structural Survey February 1992 (Unpublished typescript prepared for the Welsh Historic Gardens Trust: Lesley Howes Archaeological Services).

Howes L, 1997 *Garden Archaeology Newsletter* **1** English Heritage, London.

Hughes M, 1994 'Towns and Villages in Medieval Hampshire' in M Aston and C Lewis (eds) *The Medieval Landscape of Wessex*, 195–212. Oxbow Monograph **46**, Oxford.

Hussey C, 1967 *English Gardens and Landscapes 1700–1750* Country Life, London.

Jacques D, 1995 'The history of the Privy Garden' in S Thurley (ed) *The King's Privy Garden at Hampton Court Palace 1689–1995*, 23-42 Apollo, London.

Jacques D and van der Horst A J, 1988 *The Gardens of William and Mary* Christopher Helm, London.

Jellicoe G, Jellicoe S, Goode P and Lancaster M, 1986 *The Oxford Companion to Gardens* Oxford University Press.

Jones A G, 1970 *History of Ebbw Vale* Reprinted by Gwent Archives, 1992.

Joyner P, 1995 'Rev. John Dyer' *Carmarthens Antiquary* **31**, 56–66.

Kerkham C R, 1996 'Archaeology at Hafod: A Comment', *Garden History Newsletter* **47**, 24–6.

Kerkham C R and Briggs C S, 1991, 'A Review of the Archaeological Potential of the Hafod Demesne', *Ceredigion* **11** (1989–92), 191–210. Reprinted with additions in A E Brown (ed) *Garden Archaeology* CBA Research Report **78**, 160–74.

Klingender F, 1971 *Animals in Art and Thought to the end of the Middle Ages* Routledge and Kegan Paul, London.

Land Use Consultants, 1982a *Royal Parks Historical Survey: Hyde Park* (Report prepared for the Royal Parks Agency).

Land Use Consultants, 1982b *Royal Parks Historical Survey: Kensington Gardens* (Report prepared for the Royal Parks Agency).

Landsberg S, 1996 *The Medieval Garden* British Museum Publications, London.

Lankester R P A, 1958 *A History of Hazlegrove House in the parish of Queen Camel, Somerset* privately published, Sparkford.

Lasdun S, 1991 *The English Park, Royal, Public and Private* Vendome Press, New York.

Leach P, 1974 'The architecture of Daniel Garrett' (3 parts) *Country Life* **156**, 694–7, 766–9 and 834–7.

Leslie M, 1993 'An English landscape garden before "the English landscape garden"?' *Journal of Garden History* **13**, Nos 1/2, 3–15.

Linford N, 1993 *Geophysical survey at Reigate Priory, Surrey* Ancient Monuments Laboratory Report Series **44/93**

1997 *Geophysical Survey at Hamstead Marshall, Berkshire* Ancient Monuments Laboratory Report Series **2/97**.

(forthcoming) *Geophysical survey at Camber Castle, East Sussex, July 1996* Ancient Monuments Laboratory Report Series.

Ludlow N D, 1995 *Middleton Hall: initial assessment of the archaeological implications of the proposed Botanic garden* (Unpublished report by Dyfed Archaeological Trust for Middleton Botanic Garden/Dyfed County Council; DAT Project Record no 31018, September 1995).

Mackay D and Bowden M, 1994 *Whorlton Castle, Holy Cross church, Whorlton village and environs* (RCHME Archaeological Survey Report incorporating Corbett 1994, in the National Monuments Record).

Marshall W, 1804 *On the Landed Property of England* London.

Martin E and Oswald A, 1996 'The house and garden at Combs Hall, Stowmarket' *Proceedings of the Suffolk Institute of Archaeology* **38 pt 4**, 409–27.

McOmish D and Field D, 1994 'A survey of the earthworks on St Ann's Hill, Chertsey' *Surrey Archaeological Collections* **82**, 223–4.

Morgan G, 1997 *The Vaughans of Trawscoed: a study of the Vaughan Family and Estate through seven centuries* Gomer Press.

Morriss R K, 1990 *Clun Castle, Shropshire. An outline history* Hereford Archaeology Series **69**.

Munby J, 1993 *Stokesay Castle* English Heritage London.

Murphy K, 1997 Review of the Register of Landscapes, Parks and Gardens of Special Historic Interest in Wales, Part 1: Parks and Gardens. Gwent and Clwyd; Part 2: Landscapes Cadw: Welsh Historic Monuments, Cardiff, 1994 in *Welsh Historical Review* **18**, 543–5.

Murphy K and Ramsey R, 1996 *Hafod: The Ladies Walk, Alpine Meadow Section. Archaeological Investigation.* (Unpublished report for the Hafod Trust by Dyfed Archaeological Trust, project record no 32112).

Murphy P L and Wiltshire E J, 1994 *A Guide to sampling archaeological deposits for environmental analysis* (Unpublished notes for circulation to English Heritage contractors).

Musson C R, 1994 *Wales from the Air: Patterns of Past and Present* RCAHMW, Aberystwyth.

Myres J N L, 1932 'Three unrecognised castle mounds at Hamstead Marshall' *Transactions of the Newbury and District Field Club* **6**, 114–26.

Nenk B S, Margeson S and Hurley M, 1993 'Medieval Britain and Ireland in 1992' *Medieval Archaeology* **37**, 240–313.

Oswald A, 1954 'Ebberston Hall, Yorkshire' *Country Life* **144**, 1158–63, 1254–7.

Papworth M, 1994 'Lodge farm, Kingston Lacy Estate, Dorset' *Journal of the British Archaeological Association* **147**, 57–121.

Parsons C, 1948 'Horseheath Hall and its owners' *Proceedings of the Cambridge Antiquarian Society* **41**, 1–49.

Pattison P, 1992 'Oldstone: a mansion and its garden in South Devon' *Proceedings of the Devon Archaeological Society* **50** 125–36.

Percy V and Jackson-Stops G, 1974 'The travel journals of the 1st Duchess of Northumberland' (3 parts) *Country Life* **154**, 192–5, 250–2 and 308–10.

Pevsner N, 1966 *The Buildings of England: Yorkshire The North Riding* Penguin, London.

Pevsner N, 1989 *The Buildings of England: South and West Somerset* Penguin, London.

Pevsner N and Lloyd D, 1967 *The Buildings of England: Hampshire and the Isle of Wight* Penguin, Harmondsworth.

Phibbs J L, 1991 'Tredegar House' *Garden History Newsletter* **31**, 34–5.

1993 'Pleasure Grounds in Sweden and their English Models' *Garden History* **21 pt 1**, 60–90.

1994 *The Assassination of Capability Brown* (Working paper from Debois Landscape Survey Group).

Purdue J, Pate N and Murphy K, 1995 *Phase I and II Archaeological Evaluation at Aberglasney House, Carmarthenshire* (Unpublished report: Project Record No. 30890: Dyfed Archaeological Trust Ltd).

Rackham O, 1986 *The History of the Countryside* Dent, London.

Repton H, 1791 *Red book for Courteenhall* (Unpublished).

Reynier M J, 1994 *Excavations at the early Mesolithic site at Marsh Benham: an interim report* (Unpublished typescript, University of Nottingham).

Roberts E, 1986 *Tai Uchelwyr y Beirdd 1350–1650* Barddas.

Roberts Edward, 1986 'The Bishop of Winchester's Fishponds in Hampshire, 1150–1400' *Proceedings of the Hampshire Field Club and Archaeological Society* **42**, 125–38.

1988 'The Bishop of Winchester's Deer Parks in Hampshire, 1200–1400' *Proceedings of the Hampshire Field Club* **44**, 67–86.

1994 'The Bishop of Winchester's fishponds and deer parks' *Proceedings of the Hampshire Field Club* **49**, 229–31.

1995 'Edward III's lodge at Odiham, Hampshire' *Medieval Archaeology* **39**, 91–106.

Rocque J, 1741–5 *An exact survey of the Citys of London, Westminster, Borough of Southwark and the Country near 10 miles around.*

Rose P, 1994 'The medieval garden at Tintagel' *Cornish Archaeology* **33**, 170–82.

RCAHMS, 1929 *Tenth Report with Inventory of Monuments and Constructions in the Counties of Midlothian and West Lothian* HMSO, Edinburgh.

RCAHMW, 1937 *An Inventory of the Ancient Monuments in Anglesey* HMSO, London.

1981 *An Inventory of the Ancient Monuments in Glamorgan* **4**: *Domestic Architecture from the Reformation to the Industrial Revolution* **pt 1**: *The Greater Houses* HMSO, Cardiff.

1984 *An Inventory of the Ancient Monuments in Glamorgan* **3**: *Medieval non-defensive Earthworks* HMSO, Cardiff.

RCHME, 1968 *An Inventory of the Historical Monuments in the County Of Cambridgeshire* **1** *West Cambridge-shire* HMSO, London.

1975a *An Inventory of the Historical Monuments in the County Of Dorset* **5**: East Dorset HMSO, London.

1975b *An Inventory of the Historical Monuments in the County Of Northamptonshire* **1**: *Archaeological sites in North-East Northamptonshire* HMSO, London.

1979 *Stonehenge and its Environs* Edinburgh University Press.

1981 *An Inventory of the Historical Monuments in the County Of Northamptonshire* **3**: *Archaeological sites in North-West Northamptonshire* HMSO London.

1984 *An Inventory of the Historical Monuments in the County Of Northamptonshire* **6**: *Architectural monuments in North Northamptonshire* HMSO, London.

1994a *Greenwich Park: An Archaeological Survey* parts 1 and 2 (Unpublished survey reports).

1994b *Hyde Park: An Archaeological Survey* part 2 (Unpublished survey report).

1995 *Nonsuch Park: An Archaeological Survey* (Unpublished survey report).

Samuels A and Dixon-Hunt J, 1991 'Aberglasney: an enigmatic cloister range' *Journal of Garden History* **11**, No **3**, 131–9.

Sawyer P H, 1968 *Anglo-Saxon Charters. An Annotated List and Bibliography* Royal Historical Society, London.

Scarfe N (ed), 1988 *A Frenchman's Year in Suffolk: French Impressions of Suffolk Life in 1788* Ipswich.

Scollar I, Tabbagh A, Hesse A, and Herzog I (eds), 1990 *Archaeological Prospecting and Remote Sensing* Cambridge University Press, Cambridge.

Smith P, 1988 *Houses of the Welsh Countryside* HMSO, London.

Spiers W L, 1979 *Catalogue of the Drawings and Designs of Robert and James Adam in Sir John Soane's Museum* Chadwyk Healey, Cambridge.

Spink W, 1974 'Sir John Clerk of Penicuik: landowner as designer' in P Willis (ed) *Furor Hortensis: Essays on the History of the English Landscape Garden in Memory of H F Clark* Elysium Press Ltd, Edinburgh.

Stamper P, 1996 *Historic Parks and gardens of Shropshire* Shropshire Books, Shrewsbury.

Stawell G D, 1910 *A Quantock Family* Barnicott and Pearce, Taunton.

Steane J, 1993 *The Archaeology of the Medieval English Monarchy* Batsford, London.

Stocker D, 1993 'The shadow of the general's armchair' *Archaeological Journal* **149**, 415–20.

Stocker D and Stocker M, 1996 'Sacred profanity: the theology of rabbit breeding and the symbolic landscape of the warren' *World Archaeology* **28 pt 2** "*Sacred Geography*", 264–72.

Stokes P, 1996 *Craven Country: the story of Hamstead Marshall* P Stokes, Newbury.

Strachey J, in Somerset Record Office: DD/SH 107 Undated MSS.

Strong R, 1992 *Royal Gardens* BBC Books/Conran Octopus, London.

Stroud D, 1975 *Capability Brown* Faber & Faber, London.

Suggett R, 1995 *John Nash Architect - Pensaer* National Library of Wales/RCAHMW, Aberystwyth.

Taigel A and Williamson T, 1991 'Some Early Geometric Gardens in Norfolk' *Journal of Garden History* **11,** Nos **1/2,** 3–111.

Taylor C C, 1983a *Village and Farmstead* George Philip, London.

   1983b *The Archaeology of Gardens* Shire, Aylesbury.

   1989 'Somersham Palace, Cambridgeshire: a medieval landscape for pleasure?' in M Bowden, D Mackay and P Topping (eds) *From Cornwall to Caithness; some aspects of British field archaeology, papers presented to Norman V Quinnell* BAR British Series **209**, 211–24 Oxford.

Taylor C C, Everson P and Wilson-North W R, 1990 'Bodiam Castle, Sussex' *Medieval Archaeology* **34,** 155–7.

Thacker C, 1994 *The Genius of Gardening* Weidenfeld & Nicolson, London.

Thirsk J, 1970 'Seventeenth-century Agriculture and Social Change' in *Land, Church and People*, Supplement to the *Agricultural History Review* **18**, 148–77.

Thomas A and Morriss R K, February 1993 Old Gwernyfed, Felindre, Powys (NGR: SO 1636 1736): An Interim Report (Unpublished typescript, City of Hereford Archaeology Unit).

Thompson M W, 1964 'Reclamation of waste ground for The Pleasance at Kenilworth Castle' *Medieval Archaeology* **8**, 222–3.

   1991 *Kenilworth Castle* English Heritage, London.

Tuck C and Jecock H M, 1996 *Shotwick Castle, Cheshire* (RCHME Archaeological Survey Report, in the National Monuments Record).

Upcott K M, 1911 'Highclere' in W Page (ed) *The Victoria History of Hampshire and the Isle of Wight* **4**, 285–6 Institute of Historical Research, London.

VCH, 1906 *The Victoria County History of Berkshire* **1**.

   1924 *The Victoria County History of Berkshire* **4**.

   1925 *The Victoria County History of Buckinghamshire* **3** St Catherine's Press, London.

   1951 *The Victoria County History of Warwickshire* **4** Oxford University Press.

   1979 *The Victoria County History of Cambridgeshire* **6** Oxford University Press.

Villiers G, 1804 Letter from the Hon George Villiers at Hilfield, Aldenham in A Young *Agriculture of Hertfordshire*, 140.

Wade Martins S, 1983 *Holkham Hall: its Development Over Three Centuries* Norwich.

Walker D, 1795 *General view of the Agriculture of the County of Hertford* London.

Walpole H, 1982 *The History of the Modern taste in Gardening* New York, Garland edition.

Welfare H, Topping P, Blood K and Ramm H, 1990 'Stanwick, North Yorkshire, part 2: a summary description of the earthworks' *Archaeological Journal* **147**, 16–36.

Went D, 1986a *Caxton Moats, Cambridgeshire* (English Heritage schedule entry).

1986b *Burwell Castle, Cambridgeshire* (English Heritage schedule entry).

Wheeler R E M, 1954 'The Stanwick Fortifications, North Riding of Yorkshire' *Society of Antiquaries of London Research Report* **17**.

Whitaker T, 1823 *An History of Richmondshire in the North Riding of the County of York* (2 vols) Longman, London.

Whittle E, 1993 'Tredegar House and Raglan Castle Historic Gardens' in N J G Pounds (ed) *The Cardiff Area: Proceedings of the 139th Summer Meeting of the Royal Archaeological Institute*, 66–7, supplement to the *Archaeological Journal* **150**.

Whittle E and Taylor C C, 1994 'The early seventeenth-century garden at Tackley, Oxfordshire' *Garden History* **22 pt 1**, 37–63.

Williams-Freeman J P, 1915 *An Introduction to Field Archaeology as Illustrated by Hampshire* London.

Williamson T, 1993 *The Origins of Norfolk* Manchester University Press, Manchester.

1995 *Polite Landscapes: Gardens and Society in Eighteenth-Century England* Alan Sutton, London.

1996 'Roger North at Rougham: a Lost House and its Landscape' in C Rawcliffe, R Virgoe and R Wilson (eds) *Counties and Communities: Essays on East Anglian History presented to Hassell Smith*, 275–90. Centre of East Anglian Studies, University of East Anglia, Norwich.

(in press) *The Archaeology of the Landscape Park: Garden Design in Norfolk, England, 1660–1850* British Archaeological Reports, Oxford.

Wilson-North W R, 1993 'Stowe: the country house and gardens of the Grenville family' *Cornish Archaeology* **32**, 112–27.

1996 'Witham, From Carthusian Monastery to Country House' *Current Archaeology* **148**, 151–6.

Wilson-North W R and Cocroft W D, 1987 *Great Oxenbold, Shropshire* (RCHME Archaeological Survey Report, in the National Monuments Record).

Wilson-North W R and Porter S, 1997 'Witham, From Carthusian Monastery to Country House to Gothic Folly' *Architectural History* **40**, 81–98.

Winton H, 1994 *Witham, Somerset* (RCHME Air Photographic Transcription, in the National Monuments Record).

Yaxley D, 1994 'The Tower of Houghton St Martin Church' *The Annual Bulletin of the Norfolk Archaeological and Historical Research Group* **3**, 46–50.

Young A, 1786 *Annals of Agriculture* **5**.

1790 'Observations' *Annals of Agriculture* **14**.

1791 'A month's tour in Northamptonshire' *Annals of Agriculture* **16**.

1793 *Annals of Agriculture* **2**.

1797 *Annals of Agriculture* **28**.

www.ingramcontent.com/pod-product-compliance
Lightning Source LLC
Chambersburg PA
CBHW061302270326
41932CB00029B/3444